Rick

SNA

D0404083

Naples &
the Amalfi
Coast

CONTENTS

INTRODUCTION

This Snapshot guide, excerpted from my guidebook *Rick Steves Italy*, introduces you to Naples, Pompeii, and the Amalfi Coast. The gritty, historic port city of Naples is arguably Italy's wildest urban jungle, with a uniquely vibrant street life. Enjoy a pizza in its birthplace, and explore the city's excellent Archaeological Museum. Then head into the countryside to unearth ancient history at Pompeii and Herculaneum, well-preserved Roman towns in the shadow of the steaming Mt. Vesuvius.

An hour to the south, Sorrento kicks off the gloriously scenic Amalfi Coast, where buses filled with white-knuckle tourists take turns squeezing along an impossibly narrow sea-view road. Relax in stylish Sorrento, hilly Positano, or low-key Amalfi, and side-trip to the ancient Greek temples at Paestum, or to the jet-set isle of Capri, with its otherworldly Blue Grotto.

To help you have the best trip possible, I've included the following topics in this book:

• **Planning Your Time,** with advice on how to make the most of your limited time

• **Orientation,** including tourist information (abbreviated as TI), tips on public transportation, local tour options, and helpful hints

• **Sights** with ratings:

  ▲▲▲—Don't miss

  ▲▲—Try hard to see

  ▲—Worthwhile if you can make it

  No rating—Worth knowing about

• **Sleeping** and **Eating,** with good-value recommendations in every price range

• **Connections,** with tips on trains, buses, and driving

Practicalities, near the end of this book, has information on money, staying connected, hotel reservations, transportation, and more, plus Italian survival phrases.

To travel smartly, read this little book in its entirety before you go. It's my hope that this guide will make your trip more meaningful and rewarding. Traveling like a temporary local, you'll get the absolute most out of every mile, minute, and dollar.

Buon viaggio!

Rick Steves

NAPLES

Napoli

If you like Italy as far south as Rome, go farther south—it gets better. If Italy is getting on your nerves, don't go farther. Italy intensifies as you plunge deeper. Naples is Italy in the extreme—its best (birthplace of pizza and Sophia Loren) and its worst (home of the Camorra, Naples' "family" of organized crime).

Neapolis ("new city") was a thriving Greek commercial center 2,500 years ago. Today, it remains southern Italy's leading city. Naples impresses visitors with one of Europe's top archaeological museums (showcasing the artistic treasures of Pompeii), fascinating churches that convey the city's unique personality and powerful devotion, an underground warren of Greek and Roman ruins, fine works of art (including pieces by Caravaggio, who lived here for a time), and evocative Nativity scenes (called *presepi*). Naples, of course, makes the best pizza you'll find anywhere, and tasty pastries as well (try the crispy, ricotta-stuffed *sfogliatella*). But more than anything, Naples has a brash and vibrant street life—"Italy in your face" in ways both good and bad. Walking through its colorful old town is one of my favorite experiences anywhere in Europe.

For a grand overlook, head to the hilltop viewpoint (San Martino) for sweeping views of the city and its bay.

Naples—Italy's third-largest city, with more than one million people—has almost no open spaces or parks, which makes its position as Europe's most densely populated city plenty evident. Watching the police try to enforce traffic sanity is almost comical in Italy's grittiest, most polluted, and most crime-ridden city. But Naples surprises the observant traveler with its impressive knack for living, eating, and raising children in its streets with good humor and decency. Overcome your fear of being run down or ripped off long enough to talk with people. Enjoy a few smiles and jokes with the man running the neighborhood tripe shop, or the woman taking her daycare class on a walk through the traffic.

The pulse of Italy throbs in Naples. Like Cairo or Mumbai, it's appalling and captivating at the same time, the closest thing to "reality travel" that you'll find in Western Europe. But this tangled mess still somehow manages to breathe, laugh, and sing—with a joyful Italian accent. Thanks to its reputation as a crime-ridden and dangerous place, Naples doesn't get nearly as many tourists as it deserves. While the city has its problems, it has improved a lot in recent years. And even though it's a bit edgy, I feel comfortable here. Naples richly rewards those who venture in.

Naples is also the springboard for a full region of sightseeing treats: Just beyond Naples are the remarkable ruins of Pompeii and Herculaneum, and the brooding volcano that did them both in, Mount Vesuvius. A few more miles down the road is the pleasant resort town of Sorrento and the offshore escape isle of Capri. And plunging even farther south, you'll reach the dramatic scenery of the Amalfi Coast.

PLANNING YOUR TIME

Naples makes an ideal day trip either from Rome or from the comfortable home base of Sorrento, each just over an hour away. Or you can stow your bag at the station and see Naples in a few hours while you change trains here on the way between Rome and Sorrento. A little Naples goes a long way; if you're not comfortable in chaotic and congested cities, think twice before spending the night here. But those who are intrigued by the city's sights and street life enjoy overnighting in Naples.

On a quick visit, start with the Archaeological Museum (closed Tue), follow my self-guided Naples walk, and celebrate your survival with pizza. With more time, dip into more churches, go underground to see Greek and Roman ruins, trek to Capodimonte to see art treasures, or consider ascending San Martino for the view. Of course, Naples is huge. But even with limited time, if you stick to the prescribed route and grab a cab when you're lost or tired, it's fun. Treat yourself well in Naples; the city is cheap by Italian standards. Splurging on a sane and comfortable hotel is a worthwhile investment.

For a blitz tour from Rome, you could have breakfast on an early Rome-Naples express train (usually daily 7:35-8:45), do

Naples and Pompeii in a day, and be back in Rome in time for bed. That's exhausting, but more memorable than a fourth day in Rome.

On summer afternoons, Naples' street life slows and many churches, museums, and shops close as the temperature soars. The city comes back to life in the early evening.

Orientation to Naples

Naples is set deep inside the large, curving Bay of Naples, with Mount Vesuvius looming just five miles away. Although Naples is a sprawling city, its fairly compact core contains the most interesting sights. The tourist's Naples is a triangle, with its points at the Centrale train station in the east, the Archaeological Museum to the west, and the Piazza del Plebiscito (with the Royal Palace) and the port to the south. Steep hills rise above this historic core, including San Martino, capped with a mighty fortress.

TOURIST INFORMATION

Central Naples has multiple TIs, none of them particularly helpful—just grab a map and browse the brochures. There are TIs in the **Centrale train station** (daily 9:00-18:00, near track 23, operated by a private agency, tel. 081-268-779); by the entrance to the **Galleria Umberto I** shopping mall, across from Teatro di San Carlo (Mon-Sat 9:00-17:00, Sun 9:00-13:00, tel. 081-402-394); and along Spaccanapoli, across from the **Church of Gesù Nuovo** (Mon-Sat 9:00-17:00, Sun 9:00-13:00, tel. 081-551-2701). For information online, the best overall website is www.inaples.it. At www.inaples.it/eng/quinapoli.htm, you can download the PDF version of the monthly *Qui Napoli* booklet, which lists museum hours, events, and transportation info. A print version is occasionally available at TIs.

ARRIVAL IN NAPLES
By Train

There are several Naples train stations, but all trains coming into town stop at either Napoli Centrale or Garibaldi—which are essentially the same place, with Centrale on top of Garibaldi. Stretching in front of this station complex is the vast and gritty Piazza Garibaldi.

Centrale is the slick, modern main station. It has a small TI (near track 23), an ATM (at Banco di Napoli near track 24), a bookstore (La Feltrinelli, near track 24), and baggage check (*deposito bagagli*, near track 5). Pay WCs are down the stairs across from track 13. Shops and eateries are concentrated in the underground level.

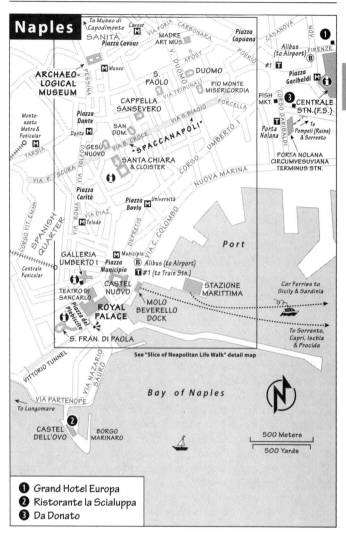

- **1** Grand Hotel Europa
- **2** Ristorante la Scialuppa
- **3** Da Donato

Garibaldi, at the lower level of the Centrale Station complex, is used exclusively by the Circumvesuviana commuter train (which you'll most likely use to connect to Sorrento or Pompeii). Note that this is not the terminus for the Circumvesuviana; that's one stop farther downtown, at the station called Porta Nolana.

Getting Downtown from the Station: Arriving at either station, the best bet for reaching most sights and hotels is either the Metro or a taxi. In the lower-level corridor (below the main Centrale hall), look for signs to **Metro** lines 1 and 2. Line 1 is handy for city-center stops, including the cruise port (Municipio), the main shopping drag (Toledo and Dante), and the Archaeological Museum (Museo). Line 2 is slightly quicker for reaching the Archaeological Museum (ride it to the Cavour stop and walk 5 minutes). For tips on navigating the Metro, see "Getting Around Naples," later.

A long row of white **taxis** line up out front. Taxi fares are fixed and should not exceed €12 or so to downtown hotels or the Archaeological Museum. If you know the going rate (ask your hotel or the TI inside the station), you're less likely to get overcharged.

By Ferry or Cruise Ship

Naples is a ferry hub with great boat connections to Sorrento, Capri, and other nearby destinations. Ferries use the Molo Beverello dock, while cruise ships use the nearby Stazione Marittima cruise terminal. The two docks are side by side at the port on the southeast edge of downtown Naples, near Castel Nuovo.

Whether arriving by ferry or cruise ship, you can get to the city center by taxi, tram, Metro, or on foot; the Alibus shuttle bus runs to the airport (see "By Plane," below).

The **taxi** stand is in front of the port area. Figure around €12 to get to the train station or to the Archaeological Museum.

If you're taking public transportation, a €1 single ticket covers either the tram or the Metro. You can buy tickets at any tobacco shop: there's one (Caffè Moreno) under the canopy between the two buildings of the cruise terminal, and another (Caffè Beverello) along the busy street. Remember to validate your ticket as you board the tram or enter the Metro station.

Tram #1 stops at the busy road directly in front of the cruise terminal and heads to Piazza Garibaldi and the train station, where you can connect to trains to sights outside of town (6/hour, 15 minutes). If you're taking the Circumvesuviana commuter line to Pompeii or Sorrento, hop off this tram a bit earlier, at Porta Nolana, where you can catch the train at its starting point.

Straight ahead across the road from the cruise terminal (on the right side of the big fortress) is Piazza Municipio, with the handy Municipio **Metro** stop. From here, Line 1 zips you right to the Archaeological Museum (Museo stop) or, in the opposite direction, to the train station (Garibaldi stop). Piazza Municipio may be torn up due to the excavation of ancient ruins found while digging the Metro station.

On foot, it's a seven-minute **walk**—past the gigantic Castel Nuovo—to Piazza del Plebiscito and the old city center. From Piazza del Plebiscito, you could do a truncated version of my self-guided walk (begin near the end of "Part 2," do that stretch backward up the hill, then launch right into "Part 3").

Planning Your Time in the Region

On a quick trip, give the entire area—including Sorrento and Naples—a minimum of three days. If you use Sorrento as your sunny springboard (see Sorrento chapter), you can spend a day in Naples, a day exploring the Amalfi Coast, and a day split between Pompeii and the town of Sorrento. While Paestum (Greek temples), Mount Vesuvius, Herculaneum (an ancient Roman site like Pompeii), and the island of Capri are decent destinations, they are worthwhile only if you have more time. For a map, see page 47.

The **Campania ArteCard** regional pass may save you a few euros if you're here for two or three days, using public transportation, and plan to visit multiple major sights (including Pompeii, Herculaneum, Paestum, Naples' Archaeological Museum, and several other museums in Naples). There are three versions of the card: The **three-day**, €32 Tutta la Regione version is good if you'll be visiting both Naples and Sorrento; it includes free entry to two sights (plus a 50 percent discount off others) and transportation within Naples, on the Circumvesuviana train, and on Amalfi Coast buses. A **seven-day**, €34 Tutta la Regione option covers five sights (and discounts on the others) but no transportation. If you're focusing on Naples, the **three-day**, €21 **Napoli-only** version covers local transportation and three city sights, plus discounts on the others (but does not cover the outlying ancient sites). You can buy the card at some Naples TIs and at participating sights (cards activate on first use, expire 3 days later at midnight, www.campaniartecard.it).

By Plane

Naples International Airport (a.k.a. Capodichino, code: NAP) is located a few miles outside of town (tel. 081-789-6111 for operator, tel. 848-888-777 for info, handy info desk just outside baggage claim, www.gesac.it). Alibus shuttle buses zip you from the airport to Naples' Centrale train station/Piazza Garibaldi in 15 minutes, and then head to the port/Piazza Municipio for boats to Capri and Sorrento (buses run daily 6:30-24:00, 3/hour, less frequent early and late, 30 minutes to the port, €3 ticket from a tobacco shop or €4 on board, stops at train station and port only). Taxi prices from the airport are fixed at generally less than €20 to most downtown hotels; insist that the driver abide by this fixed rate.

To reach **Sorrento** from Naples Airport, take the direct Curreri bus. A taxi to Sorrento costs about €100.

HELPFUL HINTS

Theft Alert: While most travelers visit Naples completely safely, err on the side of caution. Don't venture into neighborhoods

NAPLES

that make you uncomfortable. The areas close to the train station are especially seedy. Walk with confidence, as if you know where you're going and what you're doing. Touristy Spaccanapoli and the posh Via Toledo shopping boulevard are more upscale, but you'll still see rowdy kids and panhandlers. Assume able-bodied beggars are thieves.

Stick to busy streets and beware of gangs of hoodlums. A third of the city is unemployed, and past local governments have set an example that the Mafia would be proud of. Assume con artists are more clever than you. Any jostle or commotion is probably a thief-team smokescreen. To keep bags safe, it's probably best to leave them at your hotel or at the left-luggage office in Centrale Station.

Always walk on the sidewalk (even if the locals don't) and carry your bag on the side away from the street—thieves on scooters have been known to snatch bags as they swoop by. The less you have dangling from you (including cameras and necklaces), the better. Keep valuables buttoned up.

Perhaps your biggest risk of theft is while catching or riding the Circumvesuviana commuter train. At the train station, carry your own bags—there are no official porters. If you're connecting from a long-distance express, you'll be going from a relatively secure compartment into an often crowded and dingy train, where disoriented tourists with luggage delicately mix with the residents of Naples' most down-and-out districts. It's prime hunting ground for thieves. While I ride the Circumvesuviana comfortably and safely, each year I hear of many travelers who get ripped off on this ride. You won't be mugged—but you may be conned or pickpocketed. Be ready for this very common trick: A team of thieves blocks the door at a stop, pretending it's stuck. While everyone rushes to try to open it, an accomplice picks their pockets. Especially late at night, the Circumvesuviana train is plagued by intimidating ruffians. For maximum safety and peace of mind, sit in the front car, where the driver will double as your protector, and avoid riding it after dark.

Traffic Safety: In Naples, red lights are discretionary, and pedestrians need to be wary, particularly of motor scooters. Even on "pedestrian" streets, stay alert to avoid being sideswiped by scooters that nudge their way through the crowds. Keep children close. Smart tourists jaywalk in the shadow of bold locals, who generally ignore crosswalks. Wait for a break in traffic, cross with confidence, and make eye contact with approaching drivers. The traffic will stop.

Bookstore: La Feltrinelli, conveniently located in Centrale Sta-

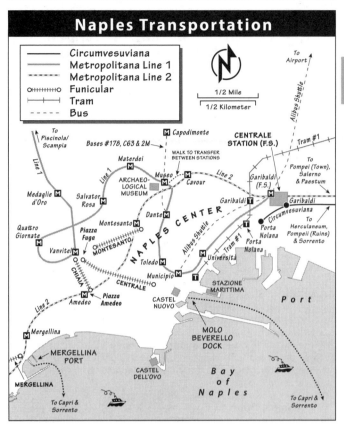

tion, carries a small selection of English-language books (daily 7:00-21:00, near track 24).

Laundry: Laundry DIY, between Piazza Dante and the Archaeological Museum, will—despite its name—do your laundry for you (€8/load, Mon-Fri 8:00-19:00, Sat 8:00-13:00, closed Sun, Via Vincenzo Bellini 50, mobile 339-318-0876).

GETTING AROUND NAPLES

Naples' entire public transportation system—Metro, buses, funicular railways, and the single tram line—uses the same tickets, which must be stamped as you enter (in the yellow machines). A €1 single ticket *(corsa singola)* covers any ride on one mode of transportation (bus, tram, funicular, or Metro line 1), with no transfers; Metro line 2 has its own €1.20 version. If you need to transfer, buy the €1.50 *90 minuti* ticket. Tickets are sold at *tabacchi* stores, some newsstands, and occasionally at station windows; Metro stations have clunky coin-op machines. A *giornaliero* day

Mondo Guide's Tours of Pompeii, Naples, the Amalfi Coast, and Capri for My Readers

Mondo Guide, a big Naples-based company, offers "shared tours" for Rick Steves readers. These allow you the luxury of a private, professional guide at a fraction of the usual cost, because you'll be sharing the expense with other travelers using this book. Their tours, which run from April through October, include **Pompeii**, a walking tour of **Naples**, and two longer-distance trips from Sorrento: an **Amalfi Coast** van tour and a private boat to the **Isle of Capri**. They also offer shore excursions for cruise passengers arriving in Naples or Salerno. I don't receive a cut from the tours; I set this up with Mondo Guide to help my readers have the most economical experience in this region.

Reservations are required. For specifics and to sign up, see their website, www.mondoguide.com, and select the "Shared Tours for Rick Steves" tab (Mondo tel. 081-751-3290, mobile 340-460-5254, info@mondoguide.com). On the website, use your credit-card number to reserve a spot. You'll then pay cash for the tour. If you must cancel, email them more than three days in advance or you'll be billed.

Each tour requires a minimum of six participants. You'll be sent an email confirmation as soon as it's sure your tour will run. If there's not enough demand to justify the trip, they'll notify you three days before the departure date (giving you time to come up with an alternative plan). Confirmed departures are continually updated on the website.

Here's a brief description of the tours:

Pompeii Tour: This two-hour guided walk brings to life the ruins of the excavated city (€15, doesn't include €11 Pompeii entry but your guide will collect money and buy tickets, daily at 10:30; meet at Hotel/Ristorante Suisse, a 5-minute walk from the train station—exiting the station, turn right, pass the Porta Marina entrance, and continue down the hill to the restaurant, on the right).

Historic Naples Walk: Naples is a challenge to enjoy and un-

---

pass costs €3.50 and pays for itself with three rides, but can be hard to find; many *tabacchi* stores don't sell them. Several versions of the Campania ArteCard include free public transport in Naples, but the card doesn't work in the subway and funicular turnstiles; you'll have to show it to the staff, who will open the gate for you. For general information, maps, and fares in English, visit www.unicocampania.it. For schedules, your only option is the Italian-only site www.anm.it.

By Metro: Naples' subway, the *Metropolitana*, has three main lines *(linea)*. Station entrances and signs to the Metro are marked by a red square with a white *M*.

on this three-hour walk, a local Neapolitan guide helps
ver the true character of the city (€25; daily at 15:00;
ne steps of the Archaeological Museum—you can do the
on your own before joining your guide).

-Day Amalfi Coast Minibus Tour from Sorrento: The
ast can be complicated and time-consuming to visit on
n, making a shared eight-seat van the simplest and most
le way to enjoy the sights. This nine-hour trip will save
d money and maximize your experience. It begins in Sor-
nd heads south for the breathtaking (and lightly narrated)
several photo stops, and an hour or two on your own in
f the three main towns—Positano, Amalfi, and Ravello—be-
eturning to Sorrento. Lunch isn't included; to save time for
exploring, just grab a quick lunch in one of the towns (€50, daily
at 9:00; meet in front of Hotel Antiche Mura, at Via Fuorimura 7, a
block inland from Piazza Tasso).

Full-Day Capri Boat Trip from Sorrento: To sidestep the
hassles of taking public boats from Sorrento for a Capri side-trip,
Mondo offers a trip to the island on a small private boat (10 people maximum), which includes an early visit to the Blue Grotto sea
cave when conditions allow (€13, optional) and about four hours
of free time to explore the island on your own. After your time
on land, the boat takes you on a lightly narrated trip around the
island with drinks, snacks, and a chance to swim if the weather
cooperates (€80, daily at 8:00, pickup at hotel, may be cancelled
in case of bad weather).

Shore Excursions from Naples or Salerno: If you're arriving on a cruise ship at the port of Naples or the port of Salerno,
Mondo Guide offers an all-day itinerary that combines three big
sights in the region: a guided visit to Pompeii with an hour or two
of free time each in Sorrento and Positano (€65/person). For details, see their website.

Line 1 has several new stations that are very useful for tourists. From the Museo stop (Archaeological Museum), line 1 heads
to Dante (at Piazza Dante, between the museum and Spaccanapoli), Toledo (south end of Via Toledo, near Piazza del Plebiscito),
Municipio (at Piazza Municipio, just above the harbor and cruise
terminal), Università (the university), and Garibaldi (on Piazza
Garibaldi in front of Centrale Station). Many of the new stations
are huge and elaborate, designed by prominent architects; Naples
is proud of its "art stations," and locals are excited to tell you about
their favorite.

Line 2 (technically part of the Italian rail system) is most useful for getting quickly from the train station to the Archaeological Museum: It runs from Centrale Station to Piazza Cavour (a 5-minute walk from the Archaeological Museum); it also stops at Montesanto (top of Spanish Quarter and Spaccanapoli street, and base of funicular up to San Martino). The new **line 6** is not yet complete; it will begin at Municipio and head west—unlikely to be of much use to tourists.

By Funicular: Central Naples' three funiculars *(funicolare)* carry commuters and sightseers into the hilly San Martino neighborhood just west of downtown. All three converge near Piazza Fuga, a short walk from the hilltop fortress and monastery/museum. The Centrale line runs from the Spanish Quarter, just near Piazza del Plebiscito and the Toledo Metro stop; the Montesanto line from the Montesanto Metro stop and Via Pignasecca market zone; and the Chiaia line from near the Piazza Amadeo Metro stop.

By Bus: Buses can be handy for certain trips, such as getting to Capodimonte. But buses are crowded and poorly signed, and aren't a user-friendly option for uninitiated newcomers.

By Tram: Tram line #1 runs along Corso Garibaldi (at the other end of the big square from Centrale Station) and down to the waterfront, terminating by the ferry and cruise terminals (direction: *Stazione Marittima*). It's useful if you're connecting from boat to train, or returning to the port after finishing my self-guided walk.

By Taxi: Taxi drivers in Naples are notorious for overcharging. A short ride in town should cost €10-12. Ask for the *tariffa predeterminata* (a fixed rate). Your hotel or a TI can tell you what a given ride should cost. There are some legitimate extra charges (baggage fees, €2.50 supplement after 22:00 or all day Sun and holidays). Radio Taxi 8888 is one reputable company (tel. 081-8888).

Tours in Naples

Local Guides

Pina Esposito has a Ph.D. in ancient archaeology and art and does fine private walking and driving tours of Naples and the region (Pompeii, Capri, the Amalfi Coast, etc.), including Naples' Archaeological Museum (€60/hour, 2-hour minimum, 10 percent off with this book, mobile 338-763-4224, giuseppina.esposito20@istruzione.it).

The team at **Mondo Guide** offers private tours of the Archaeological Museum (€120/2 hours) and city (€240/4 hours), and can provide guides or drivers throughout the region (tel. 081-751-3290, www.mondoguide.com, info@mondoguide.com).

NAPLES

Walking Tours
Mondo Guide offers my readers special shared tours of Naples and of Pompeii, as well as other trips in the region. For details, see the sidebar.

Hop-On, Hop-Off Bus Tours
CitySightseeing Napoli tour buses make three different hop-on, hop-off loops through the city. Only one of these—the red line, which loops around the historical center and stops at the Archaeological Museum and Capodimonte—is particularly helpful. The bus route will give you a sense of greater Naples that this chapter largely ignores (€22, ticket valid 24 hours, infrequent departures, buy from driver or from kiosk at Piazza Municipio in front of Castel Nuovo near the port, scant recorded narration; for details, see the brochure at hotels and TI, tel. 081-551-7279, www.napoli.city-sightseeing.it). The same company offers another route, traversing the historical center in an open-top minibus (€7, €25 combo-ticket with the main route, 40-minute loop, departs in front of the Church of Gesù Nuovo).

Cruise-Ship Excursions
Mondo Guide offers shared shore excursions for my readers. For details, see the sidebar.

Convenient for cruise-ship passengers, the **Can't Be Missed** tour company takes you from the port of Naples (or the port of Sorrento) on an all-day, big-bus trip along the Amalfi Coast that also includes a stop in Sorrento and a guided tour of Pompeii (€65, meet at 8:00 in front of port, bus leaves at 8:30, returns at 17:00, Pompeii ticket extra, mobile 329-129-8182, www.cantbemissedtours.com, 10 percent discount with this book—use promo code "RICKSTEVES" on their website).

Archaeological Museum Tour

Naples' Archaeological Museum (Museo Archeologico), worth ▲▲▲, offers the best possible peek at the art and decorations of Pompeii and Herculaneum, the two ancient burgs that were buried in ash by the eruption of Mount Vesuvius in A.D. 79. For lovers of antiquity, this museum alone makes Naples a worthwhile stop. When Pompeii was excavated in the late 1700s, Naples' Bourbon king bellowed, "Bring me the best of what you find!" The finest art and artifacts

ended up here, and today, the ancient sites themselves are impressive but barren.

Orientation

Cost and Hours: €8, sometimes more for temporary exhibits, free first Sun of the month, Wed-Mon 9:00-19:30, closed Tue. Early and temporary closures are noted on a board near the ticket office. In July and August, expect many rooms to be closed due to lack of staff.

Getting There: To take the **Metro** *(Metropolitana)* from Centrale Station, follow the signs to the Garibaldi subway station (down the stairs in front of track 13). Buy a single transit ticket at the newsstand or a tobacco shop (unless you're getting a pass), and validate it in the small yellow boxes near the escalator going down to the tracks. You're looking for line 2 *(Linea 2)* trains heading in the direction of Pozzuoli (generally depart from track 4). Ride one stop to Cavour. Walk five minutes uphill through the park along the busy street. Look for a grand old red building located up a flight of stairs at the top of the block.

If taking the Metro back to Centrale Station, it's faster to catch a train in the Cavour station, rather than at the connected Museo stop (which is on a different line).

Figure on €12 for a **taxi** from the train station to the museum.

Information: The shop sells a worthwhile *National Archaeological Museum of Naples* guidebook for €12. Tel. 081-442-2149.

Tours: My self-guided tour (below) covers all the basics. For more detail, the decent audioguide costs €5 (at ticket desk). For a guided tour, book Pina Esposito (see "Tours in Naples," earlier).

Baggage Check: Bag check is obligatory and free.

Photography: Photos are allowed without a flash.

Eating: The museum has no café, but vending machines sell drinks and snacks at reasonable prices. There are several good places to grab a meal within a few blocks.

Overview

Entering the museum, stand at the base of the grand staircase. To your right, on the ground floor, are the larger-than-life statues of the Farnese Collection, starring the *Toro Farnese* and the *Farnese Hercules*. Up the stairs on the mezzanine level are mosaics and frescoes from Pompeii, including the Secret Room of erotic art. On the top floor are more frescoes, a scale model of Pompeii, and bronze statues from Herculaneum. WCs are behind the staircase.

• *From the base of the grand staircase, turn right through the door marked* Collezione Farnese *and head to the far end—walking through a rich collection of idealistic and realistic ancient portrait busts—to reach the farthest room (Sala XIII).*

Ground Floor: The Farnese Collection

The museum's ground floor alone has enough Greek and Roman art to put it on the map. This floor has nothing from Pompeii; its highlight is the Farnese Collection, a grand hall of huge, bright, and wonderfully restored statues excavated from Rome's Baths of Caracalla. Peruse the larger-than-life statues filling the hall. They were dug up in the 1540s at the behest of Alessandro Farnese (by then Pope Paul III) while he was building the family palace on the Campo dei Fiori in Rome. His main purpose in excavating the baths was to scavenge quality building stone. The sculptures were a nice extra and helped the palace come in under budget on decorations. In the 1700s, the collection ended up in the hands of Charles, the Bourbon king of Naples (whose mother was a Farnese). His son, the next king, had it brought to Naples.

• *Quick—look down to the left end of the hall. There's a woman being tied to a snorting bull.*

The tangled *Toro Farnese* tells a thrilling Greek myth. At 13 feet, it's the tallest ancient marble group ever found, and the largest intact statue from antiquity. A third-century A.D. copy of a lost bronze Hellenistic original, it was carved out of one piece of marble. Michelangelo and others "restored" it at the pope's request—meaning that they integrated surviving bits into a new work. Panels on the wall show which pieces were actually carved  by Michelangelo (in blue on the chart): the head of the woman in back, the torso of the aunt under the bull, and the dog. (Imagine how the statue would stand out if it were thoughtfully lit and not surrounded by white walls.)

Here's the tragic story behind the statue: Once upon an ancient Greek time, King Lycus was bewitched by Dirce. He abandoned his pregnant wife, Antiope (standing regally in the background). The single mom gave birth to twin boys. When they grew up, they killed their deadbeat dad and tied Dirce to the horns of a bull to be bashed against a mountain. Captured in marble, the action is thrilling: cape flailing, dog snarling, hooves in the air. You can almost hear the bull snorting. And in the back, Antiope oversees this harsh ancient justice with satisfaction.

At the opposite end of the hall stands the *Farnese Hercules.* The great Greek hero is exhausted. He leans wearily on his club (draped with his lion skin) and bows his head. He's just finished the daunting Eleventh Labor, having traveled the world, fought men and gods, freed Prometheus from his rock, and carried Atlas' weight of the world on his shoulders. Now he's returned with the prize: the golden apples of the gods, which he cups behind his back. But, after all that, he's just been told he has to return the apples and do one final labor: descend into hell itself. Oh, man.

The 10-foot colossus is a third-century A.D. Roman marble copy (signed by "Glykon") of a fourth-century B.C. Greek bronze original (probably by Lysippos). The statue was enormously famous in its day. Dozens of copies—some marble, some bronze—have been found in Roman villas and baths. This version was unearthed in Rome's Baths of Caracalla in 1546, along with the *Toro Farnese.*

The *Farnese Hercules* was equally famous in the 16th-18th centuries. Tourists flocked to Rome to admire it, art students studied it from afar in prints, Louis XIV made a copy for Versailles, and petty nobles everywhere put small-scale knock-offs in their gardens. This curly-haired version of Hercules became the modern world's image of the Greek hero.

• Backtrack to the main entry hall, then head up to the mezzanine level (turn left at the lion and go under the *Mosaici* sign).

Mezzanine: Pompeiian Mosaics and the Secret Room

Most of these mosaics—of animals, musicians, and geometric designs— were taken from Pompeii's House of the Faun. Walk into the third room and look for the 20-inch-high statue in a freestanding glass case: the house's delightful centerpiece, the *Dancing Faun.* This rare surviving

Greek bronze statue (from the fourth century B.C.) is surrounded by some of the best mosaics of that age.

A museum highlight, just beyond the statue, is the grand *Battle of Alexander,* a second-century B.C. copy of the original Greek fresco, done a century earlier. It decorated a floor in the House of the Faun and was found intact; the damage you see occurred as this treasure was moved from Pompeii to the king's collection here. Alexander (left side of the scene, with curly hair and sideburns) is about to defeat the Persians under Darius (central figure, in chariot with turban and beard). This pivotal victory allowed Alexander to quickly overrun much of Asia (331 B.C.). Alexander is the only one without a helmet...a confident master of the battlefield while everyone else is fighting for their lives, eyes bulging with fear. Notice how the horses, already in retreat, add to the scene's propaganda value. Notice also the shading and perspective, which Renaissance artists would later work so hard to accomplish. (A modern reproduction of the mosaic is now back in Pompeii, at the House of the Faun.)

Farther on, the **Secret Room (Gabinetto Segreto)** contains a sizable assortment of erotic frescoes, well-hung pottery, and perky statues that once decorated bedrooms, meeting rooms, brothels, and even shops at Pompeii and Herculaneum. These bawdy statues and frescoes—many of them once displayed in Pompeii's grandest houses—were entertainment for guests. (By the time they made it to this museum, in 1819, the frescoes could be viewed only with permission from the king—see the letters in the glass case just outside the door.) The Roman nobles commissioned the wildest scenes imaginable. Think of them as ancient dirty jokes.

At the entrance, you're enthusiastically greeted by big stone penises that once projected over Pompeii's doorways. A massive phallus was not necessarily a sexual symbol, but a magical amulet used against the "evil eye." It symbolized fertility, happiness, good luck, riches, straight A's, and general well-being.

Circulating counterclockwise through this section, look for the following: a faun playfully pulling the sheet off a beautiful woman, only to be grossed out by a hermaphrodite's plumbing (perhaps the original *"Mamma mia!";* #12); horny pygmies from Africa in action (#27); a toga with an embarrassing bulge (#34); a particularly high-quality statue of a goat and a satyr illustrating an act of sodomy

(#36); and, watching over it all with remarkable aplomb, Venus, the patron goddess of Pompeii (#39).

The back room is furnished and decorated the way an ancient brothel might have been. The 10 frescoes on the wall functioned as both a menu of services offered and as a kind of *Kama Sutra* of sex positions. The glass cases contain more phallic art.

• *So, now that your travel buddy is finally showing a little interest in art...finish up your visit by climbing the stairs to the top floor.*

Top Floor: Frescoes, Statues, Artifacts, and a Model of Pompeii

At the top of the stairs, go through the center door to enter a grand, empty hall. This was the **great hall** of the university (17th and 18th centuries) until the building became the royal museum in 1777. Walk to the center. The sundial (from 1791) still works. Look up to the far-right corner of the hall and find the tiny pinhole. At noon (13:00 in summer), a ray of sun enters the hall and strikes the sundial, showing the time of the year...if you know your zodiac.

To your left, you'll see a door marked *affreschi*. This leads to eight rooms showing off the museum's impressive and well-described collection of (nonerotic) **frescoes** taken from the walls of Pompeii villas. Pompeiians loved to decorate their homes with scenes from mythology (Hercules' labors, Venus and Mars in love), landscapes, everyday market scenes, and faux architecture. Continue around this wing counterclockwise (with the courtyard on your left) through rooms of artifacts found at Pompeii. At the far end is a scale model of Pompeii as excavated in 1879 *(plastic di Pompeii)*. Another model (on the wall) shows the site in 2004, after more excavations.

• *Eventually you'll end up back in the great hall.*

Step out to the top landing of the staircase you climbed earlier. Turn left and go down, then up, 16 steps and into the wing labeled *La Villa dei Papiri*. This exhibition shows off artifacts (particularly bronze statues) from the  Herculaneum holiday home of Julius Caesar's father-in-law. In the second room (numbered CXVI), look into the lifelike blue eyes of the intense *Corridore* (athletes), bent on doing their best. The *Five Dancers,* with their inlaid-ivory eyes and graceful poses, decorated a portico. The next room (CXVII) has more fine works: *Resting Hermes* (with his tired little heel wings) is taking a break. Nearby, the *Drunken Faun* (singing and snapping his fingers to the beat, a wineskin at his side) is clearly living for today—true to the *carpe diem* preaching of the Epicurean philosophy. Caesar's father-in-law was a fan of Epicurean philosophy, and his library—containing 2,000 papyrus scrolls—supported his outlook. Back by the entrance, check out the plans of the villa, and in the side room, see how the half-burned scrolls were unrolled and (with luck) read after excavation in the 1750s.

• *Return to the ground floor. The exit hall (right) leads around the museum courtyard and to the gift shop.*

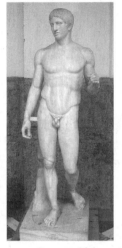

Doriforo

For extra credit on your way out, find **Doriforo.** He was last spotted on the right as you walk down the exit hall. (If he's been moved, ask a guard, *"Dov'è il Doriforo?"*) This seven-foot-tall "spear-carrier" (the literal translation of *doriforo*) just stands there, as if holding a spear. What's the big deal about this statue, which looks like so many others? It's a marble replica made by the Romans of one of the most-copied statues of antiquity, a fifth-century B.C. bronze Greek original by Polyclitus. This copy once stood in a Pompeii gym, where it inspired ancient athletes by showing the ideal proportions of Greek beauty. So full of motion, and so realistic in its *contrapposto* pose (weight on one foot), the *Doriforo* would later inspire Donatello and Michelangelo, helping to trigger the Renaissance. And so the glories of ancient Pompeii, once buried and forgotten, live on today.

Naples Walk

▲▲▲A SLICE OF NEAPOLITAN LIFE

This self-guided walk takes you from the Archaeological Museum through the heart of town and back to Centrale Station. Allow at least three hours, plus time for pizza and sightseeing stops. If you're in a rush, do it in half the time by walking briskly and skipping Part 2.

Naples, a living medieval city, is its own best sight. Couples artfully make love on Vespas surrounded by more fights and smiles per cobblestone than anywhere else in Italy. Rather than seeing Naples as a list of sights, visit its one great museum and then capture its essence by taking this walk through the core of the city.

Part 1: From the Archaeological Museum to Piazza Bellini and Piazza Dante

The first two parts of this walk are a mostly straight one-mile ramble down a fine boulevard (with a few colorful detours) to the waterfront at Piazza del Plebiscito. Your starting point is the Archaeological Museum (at the top of Piazza Cavour, Metro: Cavour or Museo; for a self-guided tour of the museum, see earlier). As you stroll, remember that here in Naples, red traffic lights are considered "decorations." When crossing a street, try to draft behind a native.

• *From the door of the Archaeological Museum, cross the street, veer right, and enter the fancy mall. (If the mall is closed for renovation, simply loop around the block to its back door.)*

Galleria Principe di Napoli: This was named for the first male child of the royal Savoy family, the Prince of Naples. Walk directly through it, enjoying this fine shopping gallery from the late 19th century, similar to those popular in Paris and London. This is "Liberty Style," Italy's version of Art Nouveau (named for a British department store) that was in vogue at a time when Naples was nicknamed the "Paris of the South." Parisian artist Edgar Degas left Paris to adopt Naples—which he actually considered more cosmopolitan and sophisticated—as his hometown.

• *Leaving the gallery through the opposite end, walk one block downhill. At Via Conte di Ruvo, head left, passing the fine Bellini Theater (also in the Liberty Style). After one block, turn right on Via Costantinopoli, continuing directly downhill to Piazza Bellini. As you walk, look up to enjoy architecture built in the late 19th century, when Naples was the last stop on Romantic Age travelers' Grand Tour of Europe. (From a tourism perspective, Sorrento only rose with the cultural and economic fall of Naples in the decades following Italian independence, around the early 20th century.)*

Soon you'll run into the ragtag urban park called...

Piazza Bellini: Walking between columns of two grand churches, suddenly you're in neighborhood Napoli. A statue of Sicilian opera composer Vincenzo Bellini, who worked in Naples in the early 1800s, marks the center of the park. Survey the many balconies—and the people who use them as a "backyard" in this densely packed city. The apartment flats were originally the palaces of noble families, as indicated by the stately family crests above grand doorways. At the downhill end of the square, peer down into the sunken area to see the ruined Greek walls: tuff blocks without mortar. This was the wall, and you're standing on land that was outside of the town. You can see the street level from the fifth cen-

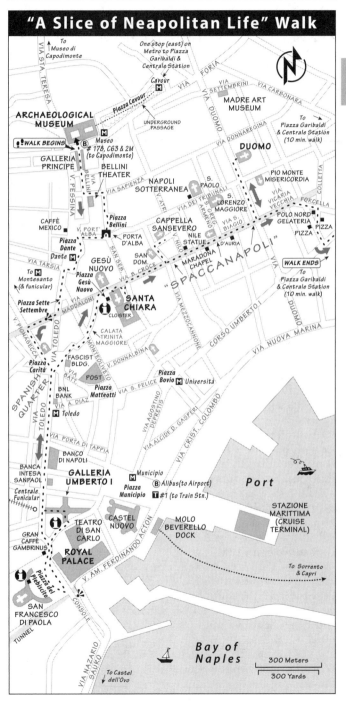

"A Slice of Neapolitan Life" Walk

tury B.C., when Neapolis—literally, "the new city"—was founded. For 2,500 years, laundry has blown in the breeze right here.

• *Walk 30 yards downhill. Stop at the horseshoe-shaped Port'Alba gate (on the right). Spin slowly 360 degrees and take in the scene. The proud tile across the street (upstairs, between the two balconies) shows Piazza Bellini circa 1890. Learn to ignore graffiti (as the locals do). Pass through the gate, and stroll past the book stalls down Via Port'Alba to the next big square...*

Piazza Dante: This square is marked by a statue of Dante, the medieval poet. Fittingly, half the square is devoted to bookstores. Old Dante looks out over an urban area that was once grand, then chaotic, and is now slowly becoming grand again.

While this square feels perfectly Italian to me, for many Neapolitans it represents the repression of the central Italian state. When Napoleon was defeated, Naples briefly became its own independent kingdom. But within a few decades of Italian unification, in 1861, Naples went from being a thriving cultural and political capital to a provincial town, its money used to help establish the industrial strength of the north, its dialect considered backward, and its bureaucrats transferred to Rome.

Originally, a statue of a Spanish Bourbon king stood in the square. (The grand orange-and-gray building is typical of Bourbon structures from that period.) But with the unification of Italy, the king, symbolic of Naples' colonial subjugation, was replaced by Dante, the father of the unified Italian language—a strong symbol of nationalism (and yet another form of subjugation).

The Neapolitan people are survivors. A long history of corrupt and greedy colonial overlords (German, Norman, French, Austrian, and Spanish) has taught Neapolitans to deal creatively with authority. Many credit this aspect of Naples' past for the strength of organized crime here.

Across the street, **Caffè Mexico** (at #86) is an institution known for its espresso, which is served already sweetened—ask for *senza zucchero* if you don't want sugar (pay first, then take receipt to the counter and hand it over). Most Italians agree that Neapolitan coffee is the best anywhere.

• *Walk downhill on...*

Via Toledo: The long, straight street heading downhill from Piazza Dante is Naples' principal shopping drag. It originated as a military road built under Spanish rule (hence the name) in the

16th century. Via Toledo skirted the old town wall to connect the Spanish military headquarters (now the museum where you started this walk) with the Royal Palace (down by the bay, where you're heading). As you stroll, peek into lovely atriums, an ancient urban design feature providing a break from the big street.

After a couple of hundred yards, you'll reach **Piazza Sette Settembre.** In 1860, from the white marble balcony of the Neo-classical building overlooking the square, the famous revolutionary Giuseppe Garibaldi declared Italy united and Victor Emmanuel II its first king. Only in 1870, a decade later, was the dream of Italian unity fully realized when Rome fell to unification forces.

• *Continue straight on Via Toledo. About three blocks below Piazza Dante and a block past Piazza Sette Settembre, you'll come to Via Maddaloni, which marks the start of the long, straight, narrow street nicknamed...*

Spaccanapoli: Before crossing the street—whose name translates as "split Naples"—look left (toward the train station). Then look right (to see San Martino hill rising steeply above the center). Since ancient times, this thin street has bisected the city. It changes names several times: Via Maddaloni (as it's called here), Via B. Croce, Via S. Biagio dei Librai, and Via Vicaria Vecchia. We'll return to this intersection later.

• *If you want to abbreviate this walk, turn left here and skip ahead to Part 3. Part 2, described next, is a bit of a detour, and requires back-tracking uphill (or a short taxi ride) later. But if you have time, it's worth the effort.*

Part 2: Monumental Naples (Via Toledo, the Spanish Quarter, and Piazza del Plebiscito)

• *We'll detour off of Via Toledo for just a couple of blocks (rejoining it later). At the Spaccanapoli intersection, go right (toward the church fa-cade on the hill, up Via Pasquale Scura). After about 100 yards, you hit a busy intersection. Stop. You're on one of Naples' most colorful open-air market streets...*

Via Pignasecca Market: Snoop around from here if you are so inclined. Then, turn left down Via Pignasecca and stroll this color-ful strip. You'll pass meat and fish stalls, produce stands, street-food vendors, and much more. This is a taste of Naples' famous Spanish Quarter, which we'll experience more of later in this walk.

• *Via Pignasecca meets back up with Via Toledo at the square called...*

Piazza Carità: This square, built for an official visit by Hitler

NAPLES

to Mussolini in 1938, is full of stern, straight, obedient lines. The big building belonged to an insurance company. (For the best example of fascist architecture in town, take a slight detour from here: With your back to Via Toledo, leave Piazza Carità downhill on the right-hand corner and walk a block to the Poste e Telegrafi building. There you'll see several government buildings with stirring reliefs singing the praises of lobotomized workers and a totalitarian society.)

In Naples—long a poor and rough city—rather than being heroic, people learn from the cradle the art of survival. The modern memorial statue in the center of the square celebrates **Salvo d'Acquisto,** a rare hometown hero. In 1943, he was executed after falsely confessing to sabotage...in order to save 22 fellow Italian soldiers from a Nazi revenge massacre.

• *From Piazza Carità, continue south down Via Toledo for a few blocks, looking to your left for more...*

Fascist Architecture (Banks): You can't miss the two big, blocky bank buildings. First comes the chalky-white BNL Bank. A bit farther down, past the Metro, imagine trying to rob the even more imposing Banco di Napoli (Via Toledo 178). Step across the street and check out

its architecture: typical fascist arches and reliefs, built to celebrate the bank's 400th anniversary (est. 1539—how old is *your* bank?).

The street here was pedestrianized after the Toledo Metro stop opened in 2012. Now the street is even more popular for strolling, property values have risen, and international brands have moved in.

• *On the next block (at #184) is the...*

Banca Intesa Sanpaolo: This fills an older palace—take a free peek at the opulent atrium. In the entry hall, you can buy a ticket for the **Galleria d'Italia Palazzo Zevallos Stigliano,** a small collection located in the upper two floors. The gallery's only piece worth seeing—on the second floor—is a great late Caravaggio painting. *The Martyrdom of Saint Ursula* shows a terrible scene: His marriage proposal rejected, the king of the Huns shoots an arrow into Ursula's chest. Blood spurts, Ursula is stunned but accepts her destiny sweetly, and Caravaggio himself—far right, his last self-portrait—screams to symbolize the rejection of evil. The rest of the second floor holds opulent chandeliered apartments, a few Neapolitan landscapes, and little else. The first floor has temporary exhibits (€5, more for special exhibits, Tue-Sun 10:00-18:00, closed Mon; entry includes audioguide, a look at old Naples paintings, and a fine WC; Via Toledo 185, tel. 800-454-229, www.palazzozevallos.com).

• *Feeling bold? From here, side-trip uphill a couple of blocks into the...*

Spanish Quarter: This is a classic world of *basso* (low) living. The streets—which were laid out in the 16th century for the Spanish military barracks outside the city walls—are unbelievably narrow (and cool in summer), and the buildings rise five stories high. In such tight quarters, life—flirting, fighting, playing, and loving—happens in the road. This is *the* cliché of life in Naples, as shown in so many movies. The Spanish Quarter is Naples at its most characteristic. The shopkeepers are friendly, and the mopeds are bold (watch out). Concerned locals will tug on their lower eyelids, warning you to be wary. Hungry? Pop into a grocery shop and ask the clerk to make you his best prosciutto-and-mozzarella sandwich (the price should be about €4).

• *Return to Via Toledo and work your way down. Near the bottom of the street, on the right at #275, is* **Pintauro,** *a takeaway bakery famous for its sfogliatelle. These classic, ricotta-filled Neapolitan pastries are often served warm from the oven and make a tasty €2 treat.*

Just beyond, on the right, notice the station for the **Centrale funicular.** *If you have extra time and enjoy city views, this can take you sweat-free up to the top of San Martino, the hill with a fortress and a monastery/museum looming over town. Across the street is the impressive Galleria Umberto I—but don't go in now, as you'll see it in a minute from the other side.*

For now, just keep heading down the main drag and through the smaller Piazza Trieste e Trento to the immense...

Piazza del Plebiscito: This square celebrates the 1861 vote (*plebiscito*, plebiscite) in which Naples chose to join Italy. Dominating the top of the square is the Church of San Francesco di Paola, with its Pantheon-inspired dome and broad, arcing colonnades.

If it's open, step inside to ogle the vast interior—a Neoclassical re-creation of one of ancient Rome's finest buildings (free, daily 8:30-12:00 & 16:00-19:00).

• *Opposite is the...*

Royal Palace *(Palazzo Reale)*: Having housed Spanish, French, and even Italian royalty, this building displays statues of all those who stayed here. Look for eight kings in the niches, each from a different dynasty (left to right): Norman, German, French, Spanish, Spanish, Spanish, French (Napoleon's

brother-in-law), and, finally, Italian—Victor Emmanuel II, King of Savoy. The statues were done at the request of V. E. II's son, so his dad is the most dashing of the group. While you could consider touring the interior, it's relatively unimpressive (described under "Sights in Naples," later).

• *Continue 50 yards past the Royal Palace (toward the trees) to enjoy a...*

Fine Harbor View: While boats busily serve Capri and Sorrento, Mount Vesuvius smolders ominously in the distance. Look back to see the vast "Bourbon red" palace—its color inspired by Pompeii. The hilltop above Piazza del Plebiscito is San Martino, with its Carthusian monastery-turned-museum and Castle of St. Elmo (remember, the Centrale funicular to the top is just across the square and up Via Toledo). The promenade you're on continues to Naples' romantic harborfront—the fishermen's quarter (Borgo Marinaro)—a fortified island connected to the mainland by a stout causeway, with its fanciful, ancient Castel dell'Ovo (Egg Castle) and trendy harborside restaurants. Farther along the harborfront stretches the Lungomare promenade and Santa Lucia district. (The long harborfront promenade, Via Francesco Caracciolo, is a delightful people-watching scene on balmy nights.)

• *Head back through the piazza and pop into...*

Gran Caffè Gambrinus: This coffee house, facing the piazza, takes you back to the elegance of 1860. It's a classic place to sample a crispy *sfogliatella* pastry, or perhaps the mushroom-shaped, rum-soaked bread-like cakes called *babà*, which come in a huge variety. Stand at the bar *(banco)*, pay double to sit *(tavola)*, or just wander around as you imagine the café buzzing with the ritzy intellectuals, journalists, and artsy bohemian types who munched on *babà* here during Naples' 19th-century heyday (daily 7:00-24:00, Piazza del Plebiscito 1, tel. 081-417-582).

• *A block away, tucked behind the palace, you can peek inside the Neo-classical...*

Teatro di San Carlo: Built in 1737, 41 years before Milan's La Scala, this is Europe's oldest opera house and Italy's second-most-respected (after La Scala). The theater burned down in 1816, and was rebuilt within the year. Guided 35-minute visits in English basically just show you the fine auditorium with its 184 boxes—each with a big mirror to reflect the candlelight (€6; tours Mon-Sat at 10:30, 11:30, 12:30, 14:30, 15:30, and 16:30; Sun at 10:30, 11:30, and 12:30; tel. 081-797-2468, www.teatrosancarlo.it).

Beyond Teatro di San Carlo and the Royal Palace is the huge, harborfront **Castel Nuovo,** which houses government bureaucrats and the **Civic Museum.** It feels like a mostly empty shell, with a couple of dusty halls of Neapolitan art, but the views over the bay from the upper terraces are impressive (€6, Mon-Sat 9:00-19:00, closed Sun, last entry one hour before closing, tel. 081-795-7722, www.comune.napoli.it).

Cross the street from Teatro di San Carlo and go through the tall yellow arch into the Victorian iron and glass of the 100-year-old shopping mall, **Galleria Umberto I.** It was built in 1892 to reinvigorate the district after a devastating cholera epidemic occurred here. Gawk up, then walk left to bring you back out on Via Toledo.

• *For Part 3 of this walk, double back up Via Toledo to Piazza Carità, veering right (just above the first big fascist-style building we saw earlier) on Via Morgantini through Piazza Monteoliveto. Cross the busy street, then angle up Calata Trinità Maggiore to the fancy column at the top of the hill. (To avoid the backtracking and uphill walk, catch a €10 taxi to the Church of Gesù Nuovo—JAY-zoo noo-OH-voh.)*

Part 3: Spaccanapoli Back to the Station

You're back at the straight-as-a-Greek-arrow Spaccanapoli, formerly the main thoroughfare of the Greek city of Neapolis.

• *Stop at...*

Piazza Gesù Nuovo: This square is marked by a towering 18th-century Baroque monument to the Counter-Reformation. Although the Jesuit order was powerful in Naples because of its Spanish heritage, locals

never attacked Protestants here with the full fury of the Spanish Inquisition.

If you'd like, you can visit two bulky old churches, starting with the dark, fortress-like, 17th-century **Church of Gesù Nuovo,** followed by the simpler **Church of Santa Chiara** (in the courtyard across the street). Both are described in more detail later, under "Sights in Naples."

• *After touring the churches, continue along the main drag. Since this is a university district, you'll see lots of students and bookstores. This neighborhood is also famously superstitious. Look for incense-burning women with carts full of good-luck charms for sale.*

Farther down Spaccanapoli—passing Palazzo Venezia, the embassy of Venice to Naples when both were independent powers—you'll see the next square...

Piazza San Domenico Maggiore: This square is marked by an ornate 17th-century monument built to thank God for ending the plague. From this square, detour left along the right side of the castle-like church, then follow yellow signs, taking the first right and walking one block to the remarkable **Cappella Sansevero.** This Baroque chapel is well worth visiting (described later, under "Sights in Naples").

• *After touring the chapel, return to Via B. Croce (a.k.a. Spaccanapoli), turn left, and continue your cultural scavenger hunt. At the intersection of Via Nilo, find the...*

Statue of the Nile (on the left): A reminder of the multiethnic makeup of Greek Neapolis, this statue is in what was the Egyptian quarter. Locals like to call this statue *The Body of Naples,* with the overflowing cornucopia symbolizing the abundance of their fine city. (I once asked a Neapolitan man to describe the local women, who are famous for their beauty, in one word. He replied simply, "Abundant.") This intersection is considered the center of old Naples.

• *Directly opposite the statue, inside of Bar Nilo, is the...*

"Chapel of Maradona": The small "chapel" on the right wall is dedicated to Diego Maradona, a soccer star who played for Naples in the 1980s. Locals consider soccer almost a religion, and this guy was practically a deity. You can even see a "hair of Diego" and a teardrop from the city when he went to another team for more money. Unfortunately, his reputation has since been sullied by problems he's had with organized crime, drugs, and police. Perhaps inspired by Maradona's example, the coffee bar has posted a quadrilingual sign (though, strangely, not in English) threatening that those who take a picture without buying a cup of coffee may find their camera damaged...*Capisce?*

• *As you continue, you'll begin to see shops selling...*

Presepi (Nativity Scenes) and *Corno*: Just as many Americans keep an eye out year-round for Christmas-tree ornaments, Italians regularly add pieces to the family *presepe,* the centerpiece of their holiday decorations. Stop after a few blocks at the tiny square, where Via San Gregorio Armeno leads left into a colorful district with the highest concentration of shops selling fantastic *presepi* and their tiny components, including figurines caricaturing local politicians and celebrities. Some even move around.

Another popular Naples souvenir that you'll see sold here—and all over the city—is the *corno*, a skinny, twisted, red horn that resembles a chili pepper. The *corno* comes with a double symbolism for fertility: It's a horn of plenty, and it's also a phallic symbol turned upside-down. Neapolitans explain that fertility isn't sexual; it provides the greatest gift a person can give—life—and it ensures that one's soul will live on through the next generation. Interestingly, in today's Naples just as in yesterday's Pompeii (where bulging erections greeted visitors at the entrance to a home), fertility is equated with good luck.

By the way, a bit farther up Via San Gregorio Armeno, you'll find the underground **Napoli Sotterranea archaeological site,** along Via dei Tribunali, which also has some of the city's best **pizzerias** (both are described later).

Back on Spaccanapoli and a bit farther along, on the right at #87, the **D'Auria** shop sells some of the best-quality *presepi* in town, many of them the classy *campane* version, under a glass bell.

• *As Via B. Croce becomes Via S. Biagio dei Librai, notice the...*

Gold and Silver Shops: Some say stolen jewelry ends up here, is melted down immediately, and gets resold in some other form as soon as it cools. Look for *compro oro* ("I buy gold") signs (for example, in the window of the shop at #95)—a sign of Italy's economic tough times.

• *Cross busy Via Duomo. If you have time and aren't already churched out, consider detouring five minutes north (left) up Via Duomo to visit Naples' **Duomo;** just around the corner is the **Pio Monte della Misericordia Church,** with a fine Caravaggio painting (both described later, under "Sights in Naples"). Afterward, continue straight along Via Vicaria Vecchia. As you stroll, ponder Naples' vibrant...*

Street Life, Past and Present: Here along Via Vicaria Vec-

NAPLES

chia, the street and side-street scenes intensify. The area is said to be a center of the Camorra (organized crime), but as a tourist, you won't notice. Paint a picture with these thoughts: Naples has the most intact street plan of any surviving ancient Greek or Roman city. Imagine this city during those times (and retain these images as you visit Pompeii), with streetside shop fronts that close up after dark, and private homes on upper floors. What you see today is just one more page in a 2,000-year-old story of a city: all kinds of meetings, beatings, and cheatings; kisses, near misses, and little-boy pisses.

You name it, it occurs right on the streets today, as it has since ancient times. People ooze from crusty corners. Black-and-white death announcements add to the clutter on the walls. Widows sell cigarettes from buckets. For a peek behind the scenes in the shade of wet laundry, venture down a few side streets. Buy two carrots as a gift for the woman on the fifth floor, if she'll lower her bucket to pick them up. The neighborhood action seems best at about 18:00.

A few blocks on, at the tiny fenced-in triangle of greenery, hang out for a few minutes to just observe the crazy motorbike action and teen scene.

• *From here, veer right onto Via Forcella (which leads to the busy boulevard that takes you to Centrale Station). A block down, a tiny, fenced-in traffic island protects a chunk of the ancient Greek wall of Neapolis. Turn right here on Via Pietro Colletta, walk 40 yards, and step into the North Pole, at the...*

Polo Nord Gelateria: The oldest *gelateria* in Naples has had four generations of family working here since 1931. Before you order, sample a few flavors, including their *bacio* or "kiss" flavor (chocolate and hazelnut)—all are made fresh daily (Via Pietro Colletta 41). Via Pietro Colletta leads past two of Napoli's most competitive **pizzerias** (see "Eating in Naples," later) to Corso Umberto I.

• *Turn left on the grand boulevard-like Corso Umberto I. From here to Centrale Station, it's at least a 10-minute walk (if you're tired, hop on a bus; they all go to the station). To finish the walk, continue on Corso Umberto I—past a gauntlet of purse/CD/sunglasses salesmen and shady characters hawking stolen mobile phones—to the vast Piazza Garibaldi, with a shiny new modern canopy in the middle. On the far side is the station. You made it.*

Sights in Naples

Naples' best sights are the Archaeological Museum and my self-guided Naples walk, both covered earlier.

CHURCHES ON OR NEAR SPACCANAPOLI

These churches are linked—in this order—on Part 3 of my self-guided walk, earlier.

▲Church of Gesù Nuovo

This church's unique pyramid-grill facade survives from a fortified 15th-century noble palace. Step inside for a brilliant Neapolitan Baroque interior. The second chapel on the right features a much-adored **statue of St. Giuseppe Moscati** (1880-1927), a Christian doctor famous for helping the poor. In 1987, Moscati became the first modern doctor to be canonized. Sit and watch a steady stream of Neapolitans taking turns to kiss and touch the altar, then hold the good doctor's highly polished hand.

Continue on to the third chapel and enter the **Sale Moscati.** Look high on the walls of this long room to see hundreds of "Ex Votos"—tiny red-and-silver plaques of thanksgiving for prayers answered with the help of St. Moscati (each has a symbol of the ailment cured). Naples' practice of using Ex Votos, while incorporated into its Catholic rituals, goes back to its pagan Greek roots. Rooms from Moscati's nearby apartment are on display, and a glass case shows possessions and photos of the great doctor. As you leave the Sale Moscati, notice the big bomb casing that hangs high in the left corner. It fell through the church's dome in 1943, but caused almost no damage...yet another miracle.

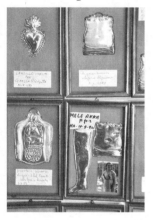

Cost and Hours: Free, daily 7:30-13:00 & 16:00-19:00, Piazza del Gesù Nuovo, www.gesunuovo.it.

Church of Santa Chiara

Dating from the 14th century, this church is from a period of French royal rule under the Angevin dynasty. Consider the stark contrast between this church (Gothic) and the Gesù Nuovo (Baroque), across the street. Inside, look for the faded Trinity on the back wall (on the right as you face the door, under the stone canopy), which shows a dove representing the Holy Spirit between the heads of God the Father and Christ (c. 1414). This is an example of the fine frescoes that once covered the walls. Most were stuccoed over during Baroque times or destroyed in 1943 by Allied bombs.

Continuing down the main aisle, you'll step over a huge inlaid-marble Angevin coat of arms on the floor. The altar is adorned with four finely carved Gothic tombs of Angevin kings. A chapel stacked with Bourbon royalty is just to the right.

Cost and Hours: Free, daily 7:30-13:00 & 16:30-20:00, Piazza del Gesù Nuovo. Its tranquil cloistered courtyard, around back, is not worth its €6 entry fee.

▲▲Cappella Sansevero

This small chapel is a Baroque explosion mourning the body of Christ, who lies on a soft pillow under an incredibly realistic veil.

It's also the personal chapel of Raimondo de Sangro, an eccentric Freemason, containing his tomb and the tombs of his family. Like other 18th-century Enlightenment figures, Raimondo was a wealthy man of letters, scientist and inventor, and patron of the arts—and he was also a grand master of the Freemasons of the Kingdom of Naples. His chapel—filled with Freemason symbolism—is a complex ensemble, with statues representing virtues such as self-control, religious zeal, and the Freemason philosophy of freedom through enlightenment. Though it's a pricey private enterprise, the chapel is worth a visit.

Cost and Hours: €7, buy tickets at office at the corner, Mon and Wed-Sat 9:30-18:30, Sun 9:30-14:00, closed Tue, no photos, Via de Sanctis 19, tel. 081-551-8470, www.museosansevero.it. Good English explanations are posted throughout; when you buy your ticket, pick up the free floor plan, which identifies each of the statues lining the nave.

Visiting the Chapel: Study the incredible *Veiled Christ* in the center. Carved out of marble, it's like no other statue I've seen (by Giuseppe "Howdeedoodat" Sammartino, 1753). The Christian message (Jesus died for our salvation) is accompanied by a Freemason message (the veil represents how the body and ego are obstacles to real spiritual freedom). As you walk from Christ's feet to his head, notice how the expression on Jesus' face goes from suffering to peace.

Raimondo's mom and dad are buried on either side of the **main**

altar. To the right of the altar, marking his father's tomb, a statue representing *Despair* or *Disillusion* struggles with a marble rope net (carved out of a single piece of stone), symbolic of a troubled mind. The flames on the head of the winged boy represent human intellect—more Freemason symbolism, showing how knowledge frees the human mind. To the left of the main altar is a statue of *Modesty*, marking the tomb of Raimondo's mother (who died after his birth, and was only 20). The veiled woman fingers a broken tablet, symbolizing an interrupted life.

Raimondo de Sangro himself lies buried in a side altar (on the right). Among his inventions was the deep-green pigment used on the ceiling fresco. The inlaid M. C. Escher-esque maze on the floor around de Sangro's tomb is another Freemason reminder of how the quest for knowledge gets you out of the maze of life. This tilework once covered the floor of the entire chapel.

Your Sansevero finale is downstairs: two mysterious...**skeletons.** Perhaps another of the mad inventor's fancies: Inject a corpse with a fluid to fossilize the veins so that they'll survive the body's decomposition. While that's the legend, investigations have shown that the veins were artificial, and the models were created to illustrate how the circulatory system works.

▲Duomo

Naples' historic cathedral, built by imported French Anjou kings in the 14th century, boasts a breathtaking Neo-Gothic facade. Step

into the vast interior to see the mix of styles along the side chapels—from pointy Gothic arches to rounded Renaissance ones to gilded Baroque decor.

Cost and Hours: Free, Mon-Sat 8:30-13:30 & 14:30-20:00, Sun 8:30-13:30 & 16:30-19:30, Via Duomo.

Visiting the Church: Explore the two largest side-chapels (flanking the nave, about halfway to the transept). Each is practically a church in its own right. On the left, the **Chapel of St. Restituta** stands on the site of the original, early-Christian church that predated the cathedral (at the far end, you can pay a small fee to see its sixth-century baptismal font under mosaics and go downstairs to see its even earlier foundations; shorter hours than cathedral). On the right is the **Chapel of San Gennaro**—dedicated to the beloved patron saint of Naples—decorated with silver busts of centuries of bishops, and seven paintings done on bronze.

The cathedral's **main altar** at the front is ringed by carved wooden seats, filled three times a year by clergy to witness the Miracle of the Blood. Thousands of Neapolitans cram into this church for a peek at two tiny vials with the dried blood of St. Gennaro. As the clergy roots—or even jeers—for the miracle to occur, the blood temporarily liquefies. Neapolitans take this ritual with deadly seriousness, and believe that if the blood remains solid, it's terrible luck for the city. Sure enough, on the rare occasion that the miracle fails, locals can point to a terrible event soon after—such as an earthquake, an eruption of Mount Vesuvius, or an especially disappointing soccer loss.

The stairs beneath the altar take you to a **crypt** with the relics of St. Gennaro and (across the room) a statue of the bishop who rescued the relics from a rival town and returned them to Naples.

Pio Monte della Misericordia

This small church (near the Duomo, and run by a charitable foundation) displays one of the best works by Caravaggio, *The Seven Works of Mercy*. Upstairs is a ho-hum art gallery. The price is steep, but it may be worth it for fans of Caravaggio.

Cost and Hours: €7, includes audioguide, Thu-Tue 9:00-14:30, closed Wed, Via dei Tribunali 253, tel. 081-446-944, www.piomontedellamisericordia.it.

Visiting the Church: Caravaggio's *The Seven Works of Mercy* hangs over the main altar in a humble gray chapel. It's well lit, allowing Caravaggio's characteristically dark canvas to really pop. In one crowded canvas, the great early-Baroque artist illustrates seven virtues: burying the dead (the man carrying a corpse by the ankles); visiting the imprisoned and feeding the hungry (Pero breastfeeding her starving father—a scene from a famous Roman story); sheltering the homeless (a pilgrim on the Camino de Santiago, with his floppy hat, negotiates with an innkeeper); caring for the sick and clothing the naked (St. Martin offers part of his cloak to the injured man in the foreground); and giving drink to the thirsty (Samson chugs from a jawbone in the background)—all of them set in a dark Neapolitan alley and watched over by Mary, Jesus, and a pair of angels. Caravaggio painted this work in Naples in 1607, while in exile from Rome, where he had been sentenced to death for killing a man in a duel. Your ticket also lets you in to the foundation's sprawling but dull upper-floor museum, with some minor Neapolitan paintings.

IN THE CITY CENTER

Royal Palace (Palazzo Reale)

Facing Piazza del Plebiscito, this huge, lavish palace welcomes the public. The palace's grand Neoclassical staircase leads up to a floor with 30 plush rooms. You'll follow a one-way route (with some English descriptions) featuring the palace theater, paintings by "the Caravaggio Imitators," Neapolitan tapestries, fine inlaid-stone tabletops, chandeliers, gilded woodwork, and more. The rooms do feel quite grand, but they lack the personality and sense of importance of Europe's better palaces. Don't miss the huge, tapestry-laden Hercules Hall. On the way out, step into the chapel, with a fantastic Nativity scene—a commotion of 18th-century ceramic figurines.

Cost and Hours: €4, includes painfully dry audioguide, free first Sun of the month, Thu-Tue 9:00-20:00, closed Wed, last entry one hour before closing, tel. 848-800-288.

▲Napoli Sotterranea

This archaeological site, a manmade underground maze of passageways and ruins from Greek and Roman times, can only be toured with a guide. You'll descend 121 steps under the modern city to explore two different underground areas. One is the old Greek tuff quarry used to build the city of Neapolis, which was later converted into an immense cistern by the Romans. The other is an excavated portion of the Greco-Roman theater that once seated 6,000 people. It's clear that this space has been encroached upon by modern development—some current residents' windows literally look down into the theater ruins. The tour involves a lot of stairs, as well as a long, narrow 20-inch-wide walkway—lit only by candlelight—that uses an ancient water channel (a heavyset person could not comfortably fit through this, and claustrophobes will be miserable). Although there's not much to actually see, the experience is fascinating and includes a little history from World War II—when the quarry/cistern was turned into a shelter to protect locals from American bombs.

Cost and Hours: €10; includes 1.5-hour tour. Visits in English are offered daily at 10:00, 12:00, 14:00, 16:00, and 18:00. Bring a light sweater. Tel. 081-296-944, www.napolisotterranea.org.

Getting There: The site is at Piazza San Gaetano 68, along Via dei Tribunali. It's a 10-minute walk from the Archaeological Museum, and just a couple of blocks uphill from Spaccanapoli's statue of the Nile. The entrance is immediately to the left of the Church of San Paolo Maggiore (look for the *Sotterranea* signs).

Porta Nolana Open-Air Fish Market

Naples' fish market squirts and stinks as it has for centuries under the Porta Nolana (gate in the city wall), immediately in front of the Napoli Porta Nolana Circumvesuviana station and

four long blocks from Centrale Station. Of the town's many boister-
ous outdoor markets, this will net you the most photos and memo-
ries. From Piazza Nolana, wander under the medieval gate and take
your first left down Vico Sopramuro, enjoying this wild and entirely
edible cultural scavenger hunt (Tue-Sun 8:00-14:00, closed Mon).

Two other markets with more clothing and fewer fish are at
Piazza Capuana (several blocks northwest of Centrale Station and
tumbling down Via Sant'Antonio Abate, Mon-Sat 8:00-18:00,
Sun 9:00-13:00) and a similar cobbled shopping zone along Via
Pignasecca (just off Via Toledo, west of Piazza Carità).

Lungomare *Passeggiata*

Each evening, relaxed and romantic Neapolitans in the mood for
a scenic harborside stroll do their *vasche* (laps) along the inviting
Lungomare promenade. To join in this elegant people-watching
scene (best after 19:00), stroll about 15 minutes from Piazza del
Plebiscito along Via Nazario Sauro.

Detour out along the fortified causeway to poke around Borgo
Marinaro ("fishermen's quarter"), with its striking Castel dell'Ovo
and a trendy restaurant scene (see "Eating in Naples," later), where
you can dine amidst yachts with a view of Vesuvius. This is known as
the Santa Lucia district because this is where the song "Santa Lucia"
was first performed. (The song is probably so famous in America because immigrants from Naples sang it to remember the old country.)
Beyond that stretches the Lungomare, along Via Francesco Caracciolo. Taxi home or retrace your steps back to the old center.

MADRE

MADRE, a museum of contemporary art, displays works by Jeff
Koons, Anish Kapoor, Francesco Clemente, and other big names
in the art world. Aficionados of modern art consider it one of the
better collections in the country. Some descriptions are in English—you'll need them.

Cost and Hours: €7, free on Mon; Wed-Mon 10:00-19:30,
closed Tue, last entry one hour before closing; Via Settembrini 79,
tel. 081-292-833, www.madrenapoli.it.

ON SAN MARTINO

The ultimate view overlooking Naples, its bay, and the volcano is from
the hill called San Martino, just
above (and west of) the city center.
Up top you'll find a mighty fortress
(which charges for entry but offers
the best views from its ramparts) and
the adjacent monastery-turned-museum. While neither of these sights

is exciting in its own right, the views are. And the surrounding neighborhood (especially Piazza Fuga) has a classy "uptown" vibe compared to the gritty city-center streets below. Cheapskates can enjoy the views for free from the benches on the square in front of the monastery.

Getting There: From Via Toledo, the Spanish Quarter gradually climbs up San Martino's lower slopes, before steep paths take you up the rest of the way. But the easiest way to ascend San Martino is by funicular. Three different funicular lines lead from lower Naples to the hilltop: the Centrale line from near the bottom of Via Toledo, the Montesanto line from the Metro stop of the same name (near the top end of Via Toledo), and the Chiaia line from farther out, near Piazza Amadeo (all three are covered by any regular local transit ticket). Ride any of these three up to the end of the line. All three lines converge within a few blocks at the top of the hill—Centrale and Chiaia wind up at opposite ends of the charming Piazza Fuga, while Montesanto terminates a bit closer to the fortress and museum.

Leaving any of the funiculars, head uphill, carefully tracking the brown signs for *Castel S. Elmo* and *Museo di San Martino* (strategically placed escalators make the climb easier). Regardless of where you come up, you'll pass the Montesanto funicular station—angle right (as you face the station) down Via Pirro Ligorio, and then continue following the signs. You'll reach the castle first, and then the monastery/museum (both about 10 minutes' walk from Piazza Fuga).

Castel Sant'Elmo

While it's little more than an empty husk with a decent modern art museum, this 16th-century, Spanish-built, star-shaped fortress boasts commanding views over the city and the entire Bay of Naples. Buy your ticket at the booth, then ride the elevator up to the upper courtyard and climb up to the ramparts for a slow circle to enjoy the 360-degree views. In the middle of the yard is the likeable little Museo del Novecento, a gallery of works by 20th-century Neapolitan artists (covered by same ticket); the castle also hosts temporary exhibits.

Cost and Hours: €5, open Wed-Mon 9:00-19:00, closed Tue, last entry one hour before closing, Via Tito Angelini 22, tel. 081-229-4401.

▲San Martino Carthusian Monastery and Museum (Certosa e Museo di San Martino)

The monastery, founded in 1325 and dissolved in the early 1800s, is now a sprawling museum with several parts. The square out front has city views nearly as good as the ones you'll pay to see from inside, and a few cafés angling for your business.

Cost and Hours: €6, Thu-Tue 8:30-19:30, closed Wed, last entry one hour before closing, audioguide-€5, Largo San Martino 8, tel. 081-229-4502, cir.campania.beniculturali.it/museosanmartino/.

Visiting the Monastery and Museum: If you want to tour the place, buy your ticket and head into the complex (which has some English information). Step into the church, a Baroque explosion with beautifully decorated chapels. Around the humble cloister are a variety of museum exhibits. The Naval Museum has nautical paintings, model boats, and giant ceremonial gondolas. In an adjacent hall is an excellent collection of *presepi* (Nativity scenes), both life-size and miniature, including a spectacular one by Michele Cucinello—the best I've seen in this *presepi*-crazy city. Beyond that is the larger garden cloister, ringed with a painting gallery (with lots of antique maps and artifacts of old Naples), and an entrance to a pretty view terrace.

ON CAPODIMONTE
▲▲Capodimonte Museum (Museo di Capodimonte)
Another hilltop, about a mile due north from the Archaeological Museum, is home to Naples' top art museum. This pleasantly un-crowded collection—with lesser-known (but still masterful) works by Michelangelo, Raphael, Titian, Caravaggio, and other huge names—fills a cavernous Bourbon-built royal palace, and sits in the midst of a sprawling hilltop park overlooking Naples. While most visitors to Naples prefer to focus on the city's uniquely vibrant street life, characteristic churches, and remarkable ancient artifacts, art lovers with some time to spare find a visit to Capodimonte worth the trip.

Cost and Hours: €7.50, free first Sun of the month, Thu-Tue 8:30-19:30, closed Wed, last entry one hour before closing, audioguide-€5, Via Miano 2, tel. 081-749-9111.

Getting There: This museum is a bit harder to reach than the other sights in this chapter, but the trip is manageable. It's easiest by taxi (figure €10-12 from the town center). You can also catch the bus from the stop directly in front of the Archaeological Museum (#178, #C63, or #2M; buy ticket at a *tabacchi* before you board).

Visiting the Museum: The collection fills a gargantuan pal-ace with a sprawling art gallery—pace yourself. After buying your ticket, head up several flights of stairs to the "first" floor, where you'll begin with several of the collection's highlights, in the Gal-leria Farnese. At the far end of the first big hall is Titian's *Por-*

trait of Alessandro Farnese, the local bigwig whose family married into Bourbon royalty; later, as Pope Paul III, he was responsible for bringing great art to Naples. (To the right, you'll see Raphael's portrait of the same pope as a much younger cardinal.) In the next, smaller room, the section of an altarpiece (1426) by the early Renaissance pioneer Masaccio shows a primitive attempt at 3-D: Masaccio has left out Jesus' neck to create the illusion that he's looking down on us. Don't miss the adjoining room, with large charcoal drawings by Raphael (Moses shields his eyes from the burning bush, 1514) and Michelangelo (a group of soldiers, 1546; and *Venus and Love,* 1534).

Continuing into the Borgia Collection, look for works by Mantegna (including the *Portrait of Francesco Gonzaga,* c. 1461, a very small but finely executed profile portrait); Giovanni Bellini's *Transfiguration*; and one of many versions of Titian's *Danaë,* where—as told in the Greek myth—the central character looks up at a cloud containing the essence of Zeus, about to impregnate her. Nearby, Titian's poignant portrait of a penitent Mary Magdalene has finely detailed tears running down her cheeks (1565).

Parmigianino's *Antea* (1531-35), another of the collection's highlights, addresses us with an unblinking, dilated gaze. As we visually follow the mink around her neck, we see—in a surreal spin—that the critter's disgusting little teeth are biting into her gloved hand. In the small, darkened, adjoining room is the *Farnese Box* (*Cassetta Farnese,* 1563), a masterwork of gold decoration.

Down the main hall are two works by Pieter Bruegel the Elder: *The Parable of the Blind* (*Parabola dei Ciechi,* 1568) is a literal and darkly comic illustration of "the blind leading the blind." *The Misanthrope* (1568) suggests the pointlessness of giving up on life and becoming a hermit; cut off from the world and lost in thought, the title figure doesn't even notice that he's about to step on a thorn, or that his wallet is being stolen by a wild-eyed young man. (Hey! I saw that guy on the Circumvesuviana!)

Annibale Carracci's *Hercules at the Crossroads* (1596) presents the hero with a choice: virtue (on the left, nature and letters) or vice (on the right, scantily clad women, music, theater masks). While his foot points one way, he looks the other...his mind not yet made up.

From here on out, you'll pass through some of the opulent apartments of this building, decorated with stunning period details and furniture. One room is slathered with red frescoes, as the houses at Pompeii once were. Another, with astonishing porcelain decor, is a masterwork of *chinoiserie*—a style reflecting Europe's fascination with Chinese culture.

Circling back to where you started, head up to the second floor. You'll see a cycle of tapestries, then halls of Gothic altar-

NAPLES

pieces. Find Colantonio's painting *San Girolamo nello Studio* (c. 1445), in which the astonishing level of detail—from the words on the page of the open book, to the balled-up pages tucked away at the bottom of the frame—drives home the message: Only through complete devotion and meticulous dedication can you hope to accomplish great things...like pulling a thorn out of a lion's paw.

Farther along on this floor, you'll reach another of the museum's top pieces, Caravaggio's *The Flagellation*. Typical of his *chiaroscuro* (light/dark) style, Caravaggio uses a ribbon of light to show us only what he wants us to see: A broken Christ about to be whipped, and the manic fury of the man (on his left) who will do the whipping. This scene could be set in a Naples alley. Compare this to most of the paintings we've seen so far—of popes, saints, and aristocrats. Caravaggio was revolutionary in showing gritty real life rather than idealized scenes—helping common people to better relate to these stories. The next room is filled with Caravaggio imitators, including Artemisia Gentileschi, one of his female followers who adapted his style for her own use (in this case, the gruesome murder of a man by a woman).

Nearby: Capodimonte is separated from Naples' town center by the gritty **Sanità** district. One of Naples' most historic and colorful zones, Sanità is sometimes called "the living *presepe*" for the way people live stacked on top of each other in rustic conditions like an elaborate manger scene. Sanità has several important churches, including some with catacombs that you can tour (because this district was just outside the city walls, the dead were buried here; for details, see www.catacombedinapoli.it). The main road from the Archaeological Museum to Capodimonte passes above this district on a Napoleon-built bridge. But if you have time and curiosity, consider walking back to the town center through this vivid neighborhood.

Sleeping in Naples

As an alternative to intense Naples, most travelers prefer to sleep in mellow Sorrento, just over an hour away. But, if needed, here are a few good options. The prices listed are typical for high season (spring and late fall). In this business-oriented city, prices are particularly soft during the slow summer months (July-Sept).

$$$ Decumani Hotel de Charme is a classy oasis tucked away on a residential lane in the very heart of the city, just off Spaccanapoli. While the neighborhood is Naples-dingy, the hotel is an inviting retreat, filling an elegant 17th-century palace with 34 rooms and a gorgeous breakfast room (standard Db-€149, bigger deluxe Db-€20 more, rates soft—check website for deals, air-con,

Sleep Code

Abbreviations   (€1=about $1.10, country code: 39)
S=Single, **D**=Double/Twin, **T**=Triple, **Q**=Quad, **b**=bathroom
Price Rankings
  $$$ **Higher Priced**—Most double rooms €130 or more
   $$ **Moderately Priced**—Most double rooms €90-130
    $ **Lower Priced**—Most double rooms €90 or less
Unless otherwise noted, credit cards are accepted, breakfast is included, free Wi-Fi and/or a guest computer is generally available, and English is spoken. Many towns in Italy levy a hotel tax of €1.50-5 per person, per night (often collected in cash; usually not included in the rates I've quoted). Prices change; verify current rates online or by email. For the best prices, always book directly with the hotel.

elevator, Via San Giovanni Maggiore Pignatelli 15—from Spaccanapoli, this lane is one street toward the station from Via Santa Chiara, second floor, tel. 081-551-8188, www.decumani.com, info@decumani.com).

$$$ Hotel Piazza Bellini is an artistically decorated hotel with 48 stripped-down-minimalist but comfy rooms surrounding a quiet courtyard. Two blocks below the Archaeological Museum and just off the lively Piazza Bellini, it offers modern sanity in the city center (generally Sb-€130, Db-€170, less if slow, bi-level "superior" Db-€20 more, extra bed-€25, air-con, elevator, Via Santa Maria di Constantinopoli 101, close to Metro: Dante, tel. 081-451-732, www.hotelpiazzabellini.com, info@hotelpiazzabellini.com).

$$$ Chiaja Hotel de Charme, with the same owner as the Decumani (listed earlier), rents 33 rooms on the Via Chiaia pedestrian shopping drag near Piazza del Plebiscito. The building has a fascinating history: Part of it was the residence of a marquis, and the rest was one of Naples' most famous brothels (Sb-€94, smaller standard Db with interior view-€149, bigger Db with view of pedestrian street-about €20 more, air-con, elevator, Via Chiaia 216, first floor, tel. 081-415-555, www.hotelchiaia.it, info@hotelchiaia.it, Pietro Fusella).

$$ Art Resort Galleria Umberto has 15 rooms in two different buildings inside the Umberto I shopping gallery at the bottom of Via Toledo, just off Piazza del Plebiscito. This genteel-feeling place gilds the lily, with an aristocratic setting and decor but older bathrooms. Consider paying €20 extra for a room overlooking the gallery (cheapest non-view Db-€115, air-con, elevator, Galleria Umberto 83, fourth floor—ask at booth for coin to operate elevator if needed, tel. 081-497-6224, www.artresortgalleriaumberto.it, info@artresortgalleriaumberto.it).

NAPLES

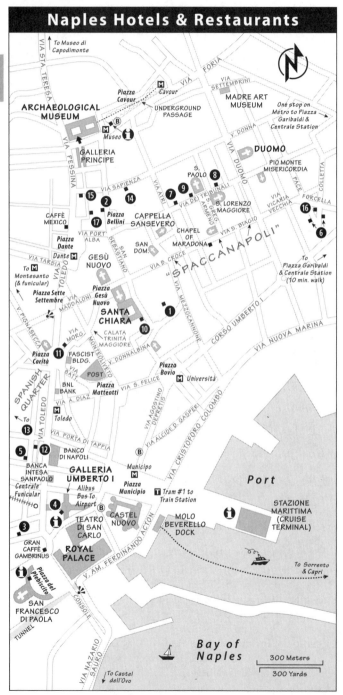

Naples Hotels & Restaurants

To Museo di Capodimonte

Piazza Cavour

M Cavour

UNDERGROUND PASSAGE

ARCHAEOLOGICAL MUSEUM

MADRE ART MUSEUM

One stop on Metro to Piazza Garibaldi & Centrale Station

B M Museo i

V. DONNA

DUOMO

GALLERIA PRINCIPE

VIA SAPIENZA

S. PAOLO 8

PIO MONTE MISERICORDIA

CAFFÈ MEXICO

15

2

14

7 9

S. LORENZO MAGGIORE

VIA VICARIA VECCHIA

16

Piazza Bellini

17

CAPPELLA SANSEVERO

CHAPEL OF MARADONA

6

VIA PORT ALBA

Piazza Dante

M Dante

GESÙ NUOVO

SAN DOM.

"SPACCANAPOLI"

To Piazza Garibaldi & Centrale Station (10 min. walk)

To M Montesanto (& funicular)

Piazza Sette Settembre

Piazza Gesù Nuovo

SANTA CHIARA

1

CORSO UMBERTO I

VIA NUOVA MARINA

VIA MORG.

CALATA TRINITÀ MAGGIORE

10

Piazza Carità

11

FASCIST BLDG.

POST

Piazza Bovio

M Università

SPANISH QUARTER

BNL BANK

Piazza Matteotti

VIA S. FELICE

To

VIA A. DIAZ

13

M Toledo

VIA PORTA DI TAPPIA

B

5

12

BANCA INTESA SANPAOLO

BANCO DI NAPOLI

Municipio

M

Port

Centrale Funicular

GALLERIA UMBERTO I

Alibus Bus To Airport

Piazza Municipio

Tram #1 to Train Station

STAZIONE MARITTIMA (CRUISE TERMINAL)

3

4

TEATRO DI SAN CARLO

CASTEL NUOVO

MOLO BEVERELLO DOCK

i

GRAN CAFFÈ GAMBRINUS

ROYAL PALACE

To Sorrento & Capri

i Piazza del Plebiscito

SAN FRANCESCO DI PAOLA

TUNNEL

Bay of Naples

300 Meters

300 Yards

To Castel dell'Ovo

Naples Hotels & Restaurants Key

❶ Decumani Hotel de Charme

❷ Hotel Piazza Bellini &
La Stanza del Gusto

❸ Chiaja Hotel de Charme

❹ Art Resort Galleria Umberto

❺ Hotel Il Convento

❻ Antica Pizzeria da Michele &
Pizzeria Trianon

❼ Gino Sorbillo Pizzeria

❽ Pizzeria di Matteo

❾ Pizzeria I Decumani &
Trattoria Campagnola

❿ Ecomesarà

⓫ Osteria il Garum

⓬ Valù

⓭ To Trattoria da Nennella

⓮ La Cantina di Via Sapienza

⓯ Caffetteria Angela

⓰ Polo Nord Gelateria

⓱ Laundry

$$ Hotel Il Convento, with 14 small but comfortable rooms with balconies, is a good choice for those who want to sleep in the gnarly, tight tangle of lanes called the Spanish Quarter—quintessential Naples. While the neighborhood can feel off-putting after dark, it's not especially unsafe. You're only a couple of short blocks off the main Via Toledo drag, and heavy-duty windows help block out some—but not all—of the scooter noise and church bells. A rare haven in this characteristic corner of town, it's in all the guidebooks (small Db-€80, Db-€110, Tb-€120, Qb-€150, €10-20 less if you prepay, air-con, elevator, Via Speranzella 137A, tel. 081-403-977, www.hotelilconvento.com, info@hotelilconvento.com).

Near the Train Station: **$ Grand Hotel Europa,** a gem on a seedy street right next to the station, has 89 decent rooms whimsically decorated with not-quite-right reproductions of famous paintings. While this location is less convenient for sightseeing and dining, it's handy for train travelers (Sb-€60, Db-€75, Tb-€90, book directly with the hotel and ask for 15 percent Rick Steves discount off these prices or check website for special deals, air-con, elevator, restaurant, Corso Meridionale 14, across street from station's north exit near track 5, tel. 081-267-511, www.grandhoteleuropa.com, booking@grandhoteleuropa.com, well-run by Claudio).

Eating in Naples

CHEAP AND FAMOUS PIZZA

Naples is the birthplace of pizza. Its pizzerias bake just the right combination of fresh dough (soft and chewy, as opposed to Roman-style, which is thin and crispy), mozzarella, and tomatoes in traditional wood-burning ovens. You can head for the famous, venerable places (I've listed five below), but these can

have long lines stretching out the door, and half-hour waits for a table. If you want to skip the hassle, just ask your hotel for directions to the neighborhood pizzeria. An average one-person pie (usually the only size available) costs €4-8; most places offer both take-out and eat-in, and pizza is often the only thing on the menu.

Near the Station

These two pizzerias—the most famous—are both a few long blocks from the train station, and at the end of my self-guided Naples walk.

Antica Pizzeria da Michele is for pizza purists. Filled with locals (and tourists), it serves just two varieties: *margherita* (tomato sauce and mozzarella) and *marinara* (tomato sauce, oregano, and garlic, no cheese). Come early to sit and watch the pizza artists in action. A pizza with beer costs around €7. As this place is often jammed with a long line, arrive early or late to get a seat. If there's a mob, head inside to get a number. If it's just too crowded to wait, the less-exceptional Pizzeria Trianon (described next) generally has room (Mon-Sat 10:30-24:00, closed Sun; look for the vertical red *Antica Pizzeria* sign at the intersection of Via Pietro Colletta and Via Cesare Sersale at #1; tel. 081-553-9204).

Pizzeria Trianon, across the street and left a few doors, has been da Michele's archrival since 1923. It offers more choices, higher prices (€5-8, plus a 15 percent service charge), air-conditioning, and a cozier atmosphere. For less chaos, head upstairs. While waiting for your meal, you can survey the transformation of a humble wad of dough into a smoldering bubbly feast in their entryway pizza kitchen (daily 11:00-15:30 & 19:00-23:00, Via Pietro Colletta 42, tel. 081-553-9426).

On Via dei Tribunali

This street, which runs a couple of blocks north of Spaccanapoli, is home to several pizzerias that are more convenient to sightseeing. Three in particular are on all the "best pizza in Naples" lists...as you'll learn the hard way if you show up at peak mealtimes, when huge mobs crowd outside the front door waiting for a table. **Gino Sorbillo** is a local favorite (closed Sun, Via dei Tribunali 32—don't confuse this with his relatives' similarly named places on the same street, tel. 081-446-643). At **Pizzeria di Matteo,** people waiting out front line up at the little window to snack on deep-fried goodies—*arancini* (with rice, gooey cheese, peas, and sausage), *frittatine* (balls of mac and cheese plus sausage), and *crocché* (croquettes)—for €1 apiece (sometimes closed Sun, Via dei Tribunali 94, tel. 081-455-262). **Pizzeria I Decumani** has a bit nicer seating and is perhaps less chaotic (closed Mon, facing Piazza San Gaetano at Via dei Tribunali 58, tel. 081-557-1309). Restaurants

If you want a full meal rather than a pizza, consider these options, which I've organized by neighborhood.

Near Spaccanapoli and Via Toledo

Ecomesarà serves up quality Neapolitan and *meridionale* (southern Italian) dishes, abiding by the Slow Food ethic, in a modern setting just below the Santa Chiara cloister, a long block south of Spaccanapoli. The atmosphere is mellow, modern, and international. Cristiano and his staff are happy to explain the menu (€12-15 pastas, €15-21 *secondi*, Tue-Sun 13:00-15:00 & 20:00-23:30, closed Mon, Via Santa Chiara 49, tel. 081-1925-9353).

Trattoria Campagnola is a classic family place with a daily home-cooking-style chalkboard menu on the back wall, mama busy cooking in the back, and wine on tap. Here you can venture away from pastas, be experimental with a series of local dishes, and not go wrong (€7-10 main courses, Wed-Mon 12:00-16:00 & 19:00-23:00, closed Tue, between the famous pizzerias at Via Tribunali 47, tel. 081-459-034 but no reservations).

Osteria il Garum is great if you'd like to eat on a classic Neapolitan square. It's named for the ancient fish sauce that was widely used in Roman cooking. These days, mild-mannered Luigi and his staff inject their pricey local cuisine with centuries of tradition, served in a cozy split-level cellar or outside on a covered terrace facing a neighborhood church. It's just between Via Toledo and Spaccanapoli, a short walk from the Church of Gesù Nuovo (€10-15 pastas, €16-21 *secondi*, daily 12:00-15:30 & 19:00-23:30, Piazza Monteoliveto 2A, tel. 081-542-3228).

Valù, with a modern red-and-black color scheme and a wine-bar vibe, sits sane and romantic in the colorful and rowdy Spanish Quarter just a block off Via Toledo. This *risotteria* specializes in risotto (which is not a local dish), serving 20 different variations. Choose between the interior or a few outdoor tables along a tight alley (€10-12 risottos, €8-16 meat dishes, Mon-Sat 12:30-16:00 & 19:00-24:00, closed Sun, Vico Lungo del Gelso 80, up alley directly opposite Banco di Napoli entrance, tel. 081-038-1139, www.valu.it).

Trattoria da Nennella is fun-loving chaos, with red-shirted waiters barking orders, a small festival anytime someone puts a tip in the bucket, and the fruit course served in plastic bidets. There's one price—€12 per person—and you choose three courses plus a fruit. House wine is served in tiny plastic cups, the crowd is ready for fun, and the food's good. It's buried in the Spanish Quarter. You can sit indoors or on a cobbled terrace under a trellis (Mon-Sat 12:00-15:00 & 19:15-23:15, closed Sun, leave Via Toledo a block down from the BNL bank and walk up Vico Teatro Nuovo three

Getting Around the Region

To connect Naples, Sorrento, and the Amalfi Coast, you can travel on land by train, bus, and taxi. Whenever possible, consider taking a boat—it's faster, cooler, and more scenic, and you can take coastline photos that you can't get from land. For specifics, check the "Connections" sections of each chapter. Confirm times and prices locally.

By Circumvesuviana Train: This useful commuter train—popular with locals, tourists, and pickpockets—links Naples, Herculaneum, Pompeii, and Sorrento. At Naples' Centrale Station, follow *Circumvesuviana* signs downstairs and down the corridor to the Circumvesuviana ticket windows and turnstiles (no self-service ticket machines—line up). Insert your ticket at the turnstiles and head down another level to the platforms.

Circumvesuviana tickets are covered by the Campania ArteCard (see page 7), but not rail passes. If you're heading to **Pompeii** or **Herculaneum**, take any Circumvesuviana train marked *Sorrento*—they all stop at both places (usually depart from platform 3). Sorrento-bound trains depart twice hourly, and take about 20 minutes to reach Ercolano Scavi (for the Herculaneum ruins, €1.80 one-way), 40 minutes to reach Pompei Scavi-Villa Misteri (for the Pompeii ruins, €2.60 one-way), and 70 minutes to reach **Sorrento**, the end of the line (€3.10 one-way). Express trains to Sorrento marked *DD* (6/day) reach Sorrento 15 minutes sooner (and also stop at Herculaneum and Pompeii). For schedules, see www.vesuviana.it.

On the platform, double-check with a local that the train goes to Sorrento, as the Circumvesuviana has several lines that branch out to other destinations. When returning to Naples on the Circumvesuviana, get off at the next-to-the-last station, Garibaldi (Centrale Station is just up the escalator). Back in Naples, you can use your Circumvesuviana ticket to cover all public transit within three hours of validation (no need to validate again).

Be on guard: Many readers report being ripped off on the Circumvesuviana (see "Theft Alert," page 7).

If you're going **from Rome to Pompeii,** note that a different (non-Circumvesuviana) train—run by the national rail company—goes from Rome to Naples, then continues to the ugly modern city of Pompei. But there is almost no reason to go to Pompei city, where you'll face a long walk to the actual site. It's better to simply get off at Naples' Centrale Station and transfer to the Circumvesuviana (described above). The Pompei city train station is useful only if you need to travel directly between the ruins and Salerno (roughly hourly, 20 minutes) or Paestum (4/day, 1 hour).

By Bus: Crowded SITA buses are most useful for traversing the popular Amalfi Coast; see "Getting Around the Amalfi Coast—By Bus" on page 114.

By Taxi: For €100, you can take a 30-mile taxi ride from

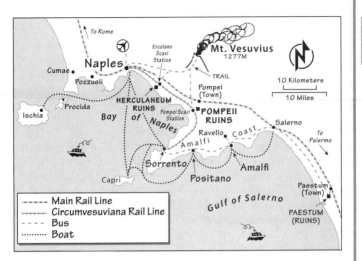

Main Rail Line
Circumvesuviana Rail Line
Bus
Boat

Naples directly to your Sorrento hotel; agree on a set price without the meter and pay upon arrival. You can hire a cab on Capri for about €70/hour. Taxis on the Amalfi Coast are generally expensive, and more than willing to overcharge you, but they can be convenient, especially with a larger group. See "Getting Around the Amalfi Coast—By Taxi" on page 116.

By Boat: Several ferry companies service the Naples, Sorrento, and Amalfi Coast areas. While these can change from year to year, major companies include Caremar (www.caremar.it), SNAV (www.snav.it), Gescab (a.k.a. NLG Jet, www.gescab.it), Navigazione Libera del Golfo (www.navlib.it), Alilauro (www.alilauro.it), and Alicost (www.alicost.it). Each company has different destinations and prices; some compete for the same trips. The quicker the trip, the higher the price. A hydrofoil, called a "jet boat," skims between Naples and Sorrento—it's faster, safer from pickpockets, more scenic, and more expensive than the train (6/day, more in summer, departs roughly every 2 hours starting at 9:00, 35 minutes). A taxi from Naples' Centrale train station to its port costs about €12-15, or you can just hop on tram #1 from across the square in front of the station.

For schedules to Capri, you can check online (www.capritourism.com; click "Shipping Timetable"), at any TI, or at Naples' Molo Beverello boat dock. Ticket windows clearly display the next available departure. The number of boats that run per day depends on the season. Trips are canceled in bad weather. Most boats charge €2 or so for luggage.

If you plan to arrive at and leave a destination by boat, note the return times—the last boat usually leaves before 19:00.

blocks to the corner of Vico Lungo Teatro Nuovo, Vico Lungo Teatro Nuovo 103, tel. 081-414-338 but no reservations).

La Cantina di Via Sapienza is a lunch-only hole-in-the-wall, serving up traditional Neapolitan fare in an interior that feels like a neighborhood joint (but has also been discovered by tourists). It's a block north of the congested, pizzeria-packed Via dei Tribunali, and a good alternative if those places are just too crowded and your heart isn't set on pizza (€5-9 meals, Mon-Sat for lunch only, closed Sun, Via Sapienza 40, tel. 081-459-078).

Near the Archaeological Museum

La Stanza del Gusto, two blocks downhill from the museum, tackles food creatively and injects crusty Naples with a little modern color and irreverence. The downstairs is casual, trendy, and playful, while the upstairs is more refined yet still polka-dotted (€7-9 *panini,* €10-18 *secondi;* fixed-price meals: €35 five-course vegetarian, €65 seven-course meat; Tue-Sat 12:00-15:30 & 19:30-23:30, closed Sun-Mon, Via Santa Maria di Constantinopoli 100, tel. 081-401-578).

Caffetteria Angela is a fun little eating complex: coffee bar; *tavola calda* with hot ready-to-eat dishes (€3-5); and a tiny meat, cheese, and bread shop with all you need for a cheap meal to go. It offers honest pricing and simple, peaceful, air-conditioned indoor seating (open Mon-Sat 7:00-21:00, Sun 9:00-14:00, 3 blocks below museum at Via Conte di Ruvo 21, between Via Pessina and Via Bellini, tel. 081-033-2928).

A Romantic Splurge on the Harbor

Ristorante la Scialuppa ("The Rowboat") is a great bet for a fine local meal on the harbor. Located in the romantic Santa Lucia district, you'll walk across the causeway to the Castel dell'Ovo in the fisherman's quarter (the castle on the island) just off Via Partenope. They boast fine indoor and outdoor seating, attentive waitstaff, a wonderful assortment of *antipasti,* great seafood, and predictably high prices. Reservations are smart (€10 pizza, €14 pastas, €18 *secondi,* Borgo Marinaro 4, tel. 081-764-5333, www.ristorantelascialuppa.net).

Near the Station

Da Donato, an excellent, traditional, family-run trattoria on a glum street near the station, serves delicious food in an unpretentious atmosphere. While you could easily make a meal of their €6-8 pastas and/or €9-15 seafood *secondi*, the best approach is for two people to share the astonishing antipasti sampler—*degustazione "fantasia" della Casa Terra e Mare*—for €25. You'll get more than a dozen small portions, each more delicious than the last. A version without seafood is €15 (Tue-Sun 12:30-14:30 & 19:30-22:00, closed Mon, Via Silvio Spaventa 39, tel. 081-287-828).

Remember, the recommended **Antica Pizzeria da Michele** (and the nearby "second fiddle" **Pizzeria Trianon**) are also relatively near the station—see descriptions earlier.

Naples Connections

From Naples by Boat to: Sorrento (6/day, more in summer, departs roughly every 2 hours starting at 9:00, 35 minutes), **Capri** (roughly 2/hour, hydrofoil: 45 minutes; ferries: 60-80 minutes); see www.snav.it and www.navlib.it. Sometimes there are also seasonal boats to **Positano** and **Amalfi**, on the Amalfi Coast—ask.

By Train to: Rome (at least hourly, 1 hour on Frecciarossa express trains; otherwise 2 hours), **Civitavecchia** (at least hourly, 3 hours, most change in Rome), **Florence** (hourly, 3 hours), **Livorno** (roughly hourly, 5 hours, most change in Rome or Florence), **Salerno** (2/hour, 35-60 minutes, change in Salerno for bus or boat to Amalfi; avoid slower trains that leave from Garibaldi Station), **Paestum** (10/day, 1.5 hours, direction: Sapri), **Brindisi** (8/day, 4.75-7 hours, overnight possible; from Brindisi, ferries sail to Greece), **Milan** (direct trains hourly, 5 hours, more with change in Rome), **Venice** (almost hourly, 5.5-7 hours with changes in Bologna or Rome), **Palermo** (2/day direct, 9-9.5 hours), **Nice** (3/day, 12 hours with change in Genoa), **Paris** (1/day, 12.5 hours with change in Turin). Any train listed on the schedule as leaving Napoli PG or Napoli-Garibaldi departs not from Napoli Centrale, but from the adjacent Garibaldi Station.

Note that the departures listed above are Trenitalia connections; Italo offers additional high-speed options to **Rome, Salerno, Florence, Milan,** and **Venice** (www.italotreno.it).

By Circumvesuviana Train: See the "Getting Around the Region" sidebar for information on getting to Herculaneum, Pompeii, and Sorrento.

To Pompeii: To visit the ancient site of Pompeii, don't use national train connections to the city of Pompei (which is far from the site). You're better off on the Circumvesuviana train, which takes you to the Pompei Scavi-Villa dei Misteri stop near the actual site.

POMPEII AND NEARBY

Pompeii • Herculaneum • Vesuvius

Stopped in their tracks by the eruption of Mount Vesuvius in A.D. 79, Pompeii and Herculaneum offer the best look anywhere at what life in Rome must have been like around 2,000 years ago. These two cities of well-preserved ruins are yours to explore. Of the two sites, Pompeii is grander, while Herculaneum is smaller, more intimate, and more intact; both are easily reached from Naples on the Circumvesuviana commuter train. Vesuvius, still smoldering ominously, rises up on the horizon. It last erupted in 1944, and is still an active volcano. Buses from the train stations at Herculaneum or Pompeii drop you a steep half-hour hike from the summit.

Pompeii

A once-thriving commercial port of 20,000, Pompeii (worth ▲▲▲) grew from Greek and Etruscan roots to become an important Roman city. Then, on August 24, A.D. 79, everything changed.

Vesuvius erupted and began to bury the city under 30 feet of hot volcanic ash. For the archaeologists who excavated it centuries later, this was a shake-and-bake windfall, teaching them volumes about daily Roman life. Pompeii was accidentally rediscovered in 1599; excavations began in 1748.

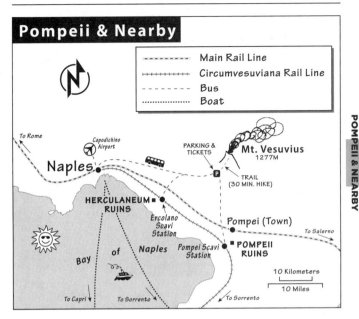

Pompeii & Nearby

- ----------- Main Rail Line
- +++++++++++ Circumvesuviana Rail Line
- - - - - - - Bus
- .... Boat

GETTING THERE

By Train: Pompeii is roughly midway between Naples and Sorrento on the Circumvesuviana train line (2/hour, 40 minutes from Naples, 30 minutes from Sorrento, either trip costs about €2.50 one-way, not covered by rail passes). Get off at the Pompei Scavi-Villa dei Misteri stop; from Naples, it's the stop after Torre Annunziata. The DD express trains (6/day) bypass several stations but do stop at Pompei Scavi, shaving 10 minutes off the trip from Naples. From the Pompei Scavi train station, it's just a two-minute walk to the Porta Marina entrance: Turn right and walk down the road about a block to the entrance (on your left).

Pompei vs. Pompei Scavi: Pompei is the name of a separate train station on the national rail network that's a long, dull walk from the ruins. Make sure you're taking the Circumvesuviana commuter train to Pompei Scavi (*scavi* means "excavations").

By Car: Parking is available at Camping Zeus, next to the Pompei Scavi train station (€2.50/hour, €10/12 hours); several other campgrounds/parking lots are nearby.

ORIENTATION TO POMPEII

Cost: €11, possibly more during special exhibits, free first Sun of each month, €20 combo-ticket includes Herculaneum (valid 3 consecutive days). Also consider the Campania ArteCard if visiting other sights in the region.

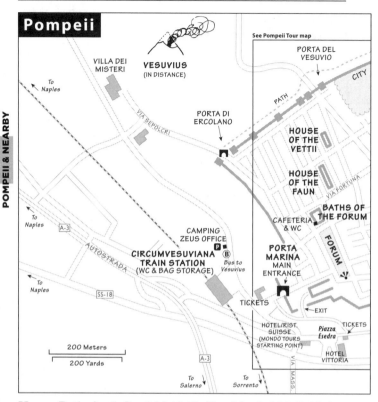

Hours: Daily April-Oct 8:30-19:30, Nov-March 8:30-17:00, last entry 1.5 hours before closing.

Closures: Be warned that some buildings and streets are bound to be closed for restoration when you visit. If you get totally derailed, just use the map and numbers to find your way.

Crowd-Beating Tip: Up to 15,000 visitors are allowed on the first Sun of the month when it's free—and packed. I'd make a point to avoid Pompeii on that day.

Information: Ignore the "info point" kiosk at the station, which is a private agency selling tours. Once at the site, pick up the free, helpful map and booklet at the entrance (ask for it when you buy your ticket, or check at the info window to the left of the WCs—the maps aren't available within the walls of Pompeii). Tel. 081-857-5347, www.pompeiisites.org.

The bookshop sells the small Pompeii and Herculaneum *Past and Present* book. Its plastic overlays allow you to re-create the ruins (€12; if you buy from a street vendor, pay no more than that).

Tours: My **self-guided tour** in this chapter covers the basics and

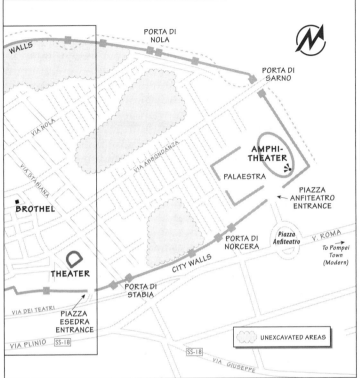

provides a good framework for exploring the site on your own, as does my 🎧 free Pompeii **audio tour.**

If you want a **guided tour,** your best bet is to join the Mondo Guide tours for Rick Steves readers (€15, doesn't include €11 Pompeii entry, daily at 10:30, reservations required, meet at Hotel/Ristorante Suisse, just down the hill from the Porta Marina entrance). Stepping off the train, you'll be accosted by touts for the "info point" kiosk, which sells €12 tours that depart whenever enough people sign up.

Private guides (around €110/2 hours) of varying quality—there really is no guarantee of what you're getting—cluster near the ticket booth at the site and may try to herd you into a group with other travelers, which makes the price more reasonable for you. Alternately, book either of the following guides in advance and mention this book. For a private two-hour tour, consider **Gaetano Manfredi,** who is pricey but brings energy and theatricality to his tours (€170 for up to 4 people, www.pompeiitourguide.com, gaetanoguide@hotmail. it). **Antonio Somma** mainly specializes in Pompeii (from €120—varies with season and number of people, also offers transport around the region, mobile 393-406-3824, tel. 081-850-1992, www.pompeitour.com, info@pompeitour.com). Parents, note that the ancient brothel and its sexually explicit frescoes are included on tours; let your guide know if you'd rather skip that stop.

Audioguides are available from a kiosk near the ticket booth at the Porta Marina entrance (€6.50, €10/2 people, ID required), but they offer basically the same info as your free booklet.

Length of This Tour: Allow two hours, or three if you visit the theater and amphitheater. With less time, focus on the Forum, Baths of the Forum, House of the Faun, and brothel.

Baggage Check: The train station offers pay luggage storage (downstairs, by the WC). Or use the free baggage check near the turnstiles at the site entrance.

Services: There's a pay WC at the train station. The Pompeii site has three WCs—one near the entrance, one in the cafeteria, and another near the end of this tour, uphill from the theaters.

Eating: The Ciao cafeteria within the site serves good sandwiches, pizza, and pasta at reasonable prices. Several mediocre restaurants cluster between the entrance and the train station. Your cheapest bet may be to bring your own food for a discreet picnic.

Starring: Roofless (collapsed) but otherwise intact Roman buildings, plaster casts of hapless victims, a few erotic frescoes, and the dawning realization that these ancient people were not that different from us.

BACKGROUND

Pompeii, founded in 600 B.C., eventually became a booming Roman trading city. Not rich, not poor, it was middle class—a perfect example of typical Roman life. Most streets would have been lined with stalls and jammed with customers from sunup to

sundown. Chariots vied with shoppers for street space. Two thousand years ago, Rome controlled the entire Mediterranean—making it a kind of free-trade zone—and Pompeii was a central and bustling port.

There were no posh neighborhoods in Pompeii. Rich and poor mixed it up as elegant houses existed side by side with simple homes. While nearby Herculaneum would have been a classier place to live (traffic-free streets, fancier houses, far better drainage), Pompeii was the place for action and shopping. It served an estimated 20,000 residents with more than 40 bakeries, 30 brothels, and 130 bars, restaurants, and hotels. With most of its buildings covered by brilliant white ground-marble stucco, Pompeii in A.D. 79 was an impressive town.

As you tour Pompeii, remember that its best art is in the Archaeological Museum in Naples (described in the previous chapter).

SELF-GUIDED TOUR
• *Just past the ticket-taker, start your approach up to the...*

❶ Porta Marina
The city of Pompeii was born on the hill ahead of you. This was the original town gate. Before Vesuvius blew and filled in the harbor, the sea came nearly to here. Notice the two openings in the gate (ahead, up the ramp). Both were left open by day to admit major traffic. At night, the larger one was closed for better security.

• *Pass through the Porta Marina and continue up to the top of the street, pausing at the three large stepping-stones in the middle.*

❷ Pompeii's Streets
Every day, Pompeiians flooded the streets with gushing water to clean them. These stepping-stones let pedestrians cross without

getting their sandals wet. Chariots traveling in either direction could straddle the stones (all had standard-size axles). A single stepping-stone in a road means it was a one-way street, a pair indicates an ordinary two-way, and three (like this) signifies a major thoroughfare. The basalt stones are the original Roman pavement. The sidewalks (elevated to hide the plumbing) were paved with bits of broken pots (an ancient form of recycling) and studded with reflective bits of white marble. These "cats' eyes" helped people get around after dark, either by moonlight or with the help of lamps.

• *Continue straight ahead, don your mental toga, and enter the city as the Romans once did. The road opens up into the spacious main square:*

the Forum. Stand at the right end of this rectangular space and look toward Mount Vesuvius.

❸ The Forum (Foro)

Pompeii's commercial, religious, and political center stands at the intersection of the city's two main streets. While it's the most ruined part of Pompeii, it's grand nonetheless. Picture the piazza surrounded by two-story buildings on all sides. The pedestals that line the square once held statues (now safely displayed in the museum in Naples). In Pompeii's heyday, its citizens gathered here in the main square to shop, talk politics, and

socialize. Business took place in the important buildings that lined the piazza.

The Forum was dominated by the **Temple of Jupiter,** at the far end (marked by a half-dozen ruined columns atop a stair-step base). Jupiter was the supreme god of the Roman pantheon—you might be able to make out his little white marble head at the center-rear of the temple.

At the near end of the Forum (behind where you're standing) is the **curia,** or city hall. Like many Roman buildings, it was built with brick and mortar, then covered with marble walls and floors. To your left (as you face Vesuvius and the Temple of Jupiter) is the **basilica,** or courthouse.

Since Pompeii was a pretty typical Roman town, it has the same layout and components that you'll find in any Roman city— main square, curia, basilica, temples, axis of roads, and so on. All power converged at the Forum: religious (the temple), political (the curia), judicial (the basilica), and commercial (this piazza was the main marketplace). Even the power of the people was expressed here, since this is where they gathered to vote. Imagine the hubbub of this town square in its heyday.

Look beyond the Temple of Jupiter. Five miles to the north looms the ominous backstory to this site: **Mount Vesuvius.** Mentally draw a triangle up from the two remaining peaks to reconstruct the mountain before the eruption. When it blew, Pompeiians had no idea that they were living under a volcano, as Vesuvius hadn't erupted for 1,200 years. Imagine the wonder—then the horror—as a column of pulverized rock roared upward, and then ash began to fall. The weight of the ash and small rocks collapsed Pompeii's roofs later that day, crushing people who had taken refuge inside buildings instead of fleeing the city.

• *As you face Vesuvius, the basilica is to your left, lined with stumps of*

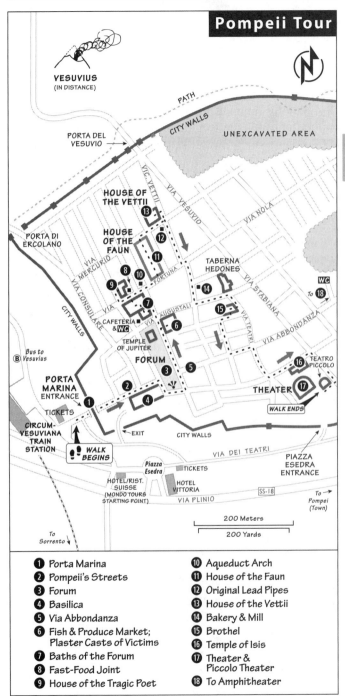

Pompeii Tour

VESUVIUS
(IN DISTANCE)

PATH

CITY WALLS

PORTA DEL
VESUVIO →

UNEXCAVATED AREA

HOUSE OF
THE VETTII

PORTA DI
ERCOLANO

HOUSE
OF THE
FAUN

VIA VETTII

VIA VESUVIO

VIA NOLA

TABERNA
HEDONES

VIA MERCURIO

VIA CONSULARE

CITY WALLS

VIA FORTUNA

VIA STABIANA

WC
To 18

VIA AUGUSTALI

VIA TEATRI

VIA ABBONDANZA

Bus to
B Vesuvius

CAFETERIA
& WC

TEMPLE
OF JUPITER

FORUM

PORTA
MARINA
ENTRANCE

TICKETS

CIRCUM-
VESUVIANA
TRAIN
STATION

WALK
BEGINS

TEATRO
PICCOLO

THEATER

WALK ENDS

EXIT

CITY WALLS

Piazza
Esedra

TICKETS

VIA DEI TEATRI

PIAZZA
ESEDRA
ENTRANCE

HOTEL/RIST.
SUISSE
(MONDO TOURS
STARTING POINT)

HOTEL
VITTORIA

SS-18

To →
Pompei
(Town)

VIA PLINIO

To
Sorrento

200 Meters

200 Yards

1 Porta Marina
2 Pompeii's Streets
3 Forum
4 Basilica
5 Via Abbondanza
6 Fish & Produce Market;
   Plaster Casts of Victims
7 Baths of the Forum
8 Fast-Food Joint
9 House of the Tragic Poet

10 Aqueduct Arch
11 House of the Faun
12 Original Lead Pipes
13 House of the Vettii
14 Bakery & Mill
15 Brothel
16 Temple of Isis
17 Theater &
   Piccolo Theater
18 To Amphitheater

columns. Backtrack to the three stepping stones we saw earlier to go in-side. (If it's fenced off, peer through the gate.)

❹ Basilica

Pompeii's basilica was a first-century palace of justice. This an-cient law court has the same floor plan later adopted by many Christian churches (which are also called basilicas). The big cen-tral hall (or nave) is flanked by rows of columns marking off nar-rower side aisles. Along the side walls are traces of the original marble.

The columns—now stumps all about the same height—were not ruined by the volcano. Rather, they were left unfinished when Vesuvius blew. Pompeii had been devastated by an earthquake in A.D. 62, and was just in the process of re-building the basilica when Vesuvius erupted, 17 years later. The half-built columns show off the technology of the day. Uniform bricks were stacked around a cylindrical core. Once fin-ished, they would have been coated with marble dust stucco to simu-
late marble columns—an economical construction method found throughout Pompeii (and the Roman Empire).

Besides the earthquake and the eruption, Pompeii's buildings have suffered other ravages over the years, including Spanish plun-derers (c. 1800), 19th-century souvenir hunters, WWII bombs, wild vegetation, another earthquake in 1980, and modern neglect. The fact that the entire city was covered by the eruption of A.D. 79 actually helped preserve it, saving it from the sixth-century barbar-ians who plundered many other towns into oblivion.

• *Exit the basilica and cross the short side of the square, to where the city's main street hits the Forum. Stop at the three white stones that stick up from the cobbles.*

❺ Via Abbondanza

Glance down Via Abbondanza, Pompeii's main street. Lined with shops, bars, and restaurants, it was a lively, pedestrian-only zone.

The three "beaver-teeth" stones are traffic barriers that kept chariots out. On the corner at the start of the street (just to the left), take a close look at the dark travertine column standing next to the white one. Notice that the marble drums

of the white column are not chiseled entirely round—another construction project left unfinished when Vesuvius erupted.

• *Head toward Vesuvius, walking along the right side of the Forum. Immediately across from the Temple of Jupiter is a building with four round arches. Go in the door just to the right, and find two glass cases.*

❻ Fish and Produce Market Plaster Casts of Victims

As the frescoes on the wall (just inside on the left) indicate, this is where Pompeiians came to buy their food—fish, bread, chickens, and so on. These fine examples of Roman art—with their glimpses of everyday life and their mastery of depth and illusion—would not be matched until the Renaissance, a thousand years after the fall of Rome.

The glass cases hold casts of Pompeiians, eerily captured in their last moments. They were quickly suffocated by a superheated avalanche of gas and ash, and their bodies were encased in volcanic debris. While excavating, modern archaeologists detected hollow spaces underfoot, created when the victims' bodies decomposed. By gently filling the holes with plaster, the archaeologists were able to create molds of the Pompeiians who were caught in the disaster.

• *Exit the market, turn right, and go under the arch. On the pillar to the right, look for the pedestrian-only road sign (two guys carrying an amphora, or ancient jug; it's above the* REG VII INS IV *sign). In the road are more "beaver-teeth" traffic blocks. The modern cafeteria is the only eatery inside the archaeological site (with a coffee bar and WC upstairs).*

Twenty yards past the cafeteria, on the left-hand side at #24, is the entrance to the...

❼ Baths of the Forum (Terme del Foro)

Pompeii had six public baths, each with a men's and a women's section. You're in the men's zone. The leafy courtyard at the entrance was the gymnasium. After working out, clients could relax with a hot bath *(caldarium)*, warm bath *(tepidarium)*, or cold plunge *(frigidarium)*.

The first big, plain room you enter served as the **dressing room.** Holes on the walls were for pegs to hang clothing. High up, the window (with a faded Neptune underneath) was originally covered with a less-translucent Roman glass. Walk over the nonslip mosaics into the next room.

The ***tepidarium*** is ringed by mini statues or *telamones* (male

The Eruption of Vesuvius

At about 1:00 in the afternoon on August 24, A.D. 79, Mount Vesuvius erupted, sending a mushroom cloud of ash, dust, and rocks 12 miles into the air. It spewed for 18 hours straight, as winds blew the cloud southward. The white-gray ash settled like a heavy snow on Pompeii, its weight eventually collapsing roofs and floors, but leaving the walls intact. And though most of Pompeii's 20,000 residents fled that day, about 2,000 stayed behind.

Although the city of Herculaneum was closer to the volcano—about four miles away—at first it largely escaped the rain of ash, due to the direction of the wind. However, 12 hours after Vesuvius awoke, the type of eruption suddenly changed. The mountain let loose a superheated avalanche of ash, pumice, and gas. This red-hot "pyroclastic flow" sped down the side of the mountain at nearly 100 miles per hour, engulfing Herculaneum and cooking its residents alive. Several more flows over the next few hours further entombed Herculaneum, burying it in nearly 60 feet of hot material that later cooled into rock, freezing the city in time. Then, at around 7:30 in the morning, another pyroclastic flow headed south and struck Pompeii, dealing a fatal blow to those who'd remained behind.

caryatids, figures used as supporting pillars), which divided the lockers. Clients would undress and warm up here, perhaps stretching out on one of the bronze benches near the bronze heater for a massage. Look at the ceiling—half crushed by the eruption and half intact, with its fine blue-and-white stucco work.

Next, admire the engineering in the steam-bath room, or *caldarium*. The double floor was heated from below—so nice with bare feet (look into the grate across from where you entered to see the brick support towers). The double walls with brown terra-cotta tiles held the heat. Romans soaked in the big tub, which was filled with hot water. Opposite the big tub is a fountain, which spouted water onto the hot floor, creating steam. The lettering on the fountain reminded those  enjoying the room which two politicians paid for it...and how much it cost them (5,250 *sestertii*). To keep condensation from dripping annoyingly from the ceiling, fluting (ribbing) was added to carry water down the walls.

• *Today's visitors exit the baths through the original entry (at the far end of the dressing room). Hungry? Immediately across the street is an ancient...*

❽ Fast-Food Joint

After a bath, it was only natural to want a little snack. So, just across the street is a fast-food joint, marked by a series of rectangular marble counters. Most ancient Romans didn't cook for themselves in their tiny apartments, so to-go places like this were commonplace. The holes in the counters held the pots for food. Each container was like a thermos, with a wooden lid to keep the soup hot, the wine cool, and so on. Notice the groove in the front doorstep and the holes out on the curb. The holes likely accommodated cords for stretching awnings over the sidewalk to shield the clientele from the hot sun, while the grooves were for the shop's folding accordion doors. Look at the wheel grooves in the pavement, worn down through centuries of use. Nearby are more stepping-stones for pedestrians to cross the flooded streets.

• *Just a few steps uphill from the fast-food joint, at #5 (with a locked gate), is the...*

❾ House of the Tragic Poet (Casa del Poeta Tragico)

This house is typical Roman style. The entry is flanked by two family-owned shops (each with a track for a collapsing accordion door). The home is like a train running straight away from the street: atrium (with skylight and pool to catch the rain), den (where deals were made by the shopkeeper), and garden (with rooms facing it and a shrine to remember both the gods and family ancestors). In the entryway is the famous "Beware of Dog" *(Cave Canem)* mosaic.

Today's visitors enter the home by the back door (circle around to the left). On your way there, look for the modern exposed pipe on the left side of the lane; this is the same as ones used in the ancient plumbing system, hidden beneath the raised sidewalk. Inside the house, the grooves on the marble well-head in the entry hall (possibly closed) were formed by generations of inhabitants dragging the bucket up by rope. The richly frescoed dining room is off the garden. Diners lounged on their couches (the Roman custom) and enjoyed frescoes with fake "windows," giving the illusion of a bigger and airier room. Next to the dining room is a humble BBQ-style kitchen with a little closet for the toilet (the kitchen and bathroom shared the same plumbing).

• *Return to the fast-food place and continue about 10 yards downhill to the big intersection. From the center of the intersection, look left to see a giant arch, framing a nice view of Mount Vesuvius.*

❿ Aqueduct Arch—Running Water

Water was critical for this city of 20,000 people, and this arch was part of Pompeii's water-delivery system. A 100-mile-long aqueduct carried fresh water down from the hillsides to a big reservoir

perched at the highest point of the city wall. Since overall water pressure was disappointing, Pompeiians built arches like the brick one you see here (originally covered in marble) with hidden water tanks at the top. Located just below the altitude of the main tank, these smaller tanks were filled by gravity and provided each neighborhood with reliable pressure.

• *If you're thirsty, fill your water bottle from the modern fountain. Then continue straight downhill one block (50 yards) to #2 on the left.*

⓫ House of the Faun (Casa del Fauno)

Stand across the street and marvel at the grand entry with *"HAVE"* (hail to you) as a welcome mat. Go in. Notice the two shrines above

the entryway—one dedicated to the gods, the other to this wealthy family's ancestors. (Contemporary Neapolitans still carry on this practice; you'll notice little shrines embedded in walls all over Naples.)

You are standing in Pompeii's largest home, where you're greeted by the delightful small bronze statue of the *Dancing Faun,* famed for its realistic movement and fine proportion. (The original is in Naples' Archaeological Museum.) With 40 rooms and 27,000 square feet, the House of the Faun covers an entire city block. The next floor mosaic, with an intricate diamond-like design, decorates the homeowner's office. Beyond that, at the far end of the first garden, is the famous floor mosaic of the *Battle of Alexander.* (The original is also at the museum in Naples.) In 333 B.C., Alexander the Great beat Darius and the Persians. Romans had great respect for Alexander, the first great emperor before Rome's. While most of Pompeii's nouveau riche had notoriously bad taste and stuffed their palaces with over-the-top, mismatched decor, this guy had class. Both the faun (an ancient copy of a famous Greek statue) and the Alexander mosaic show an appreciation for history.

The house's back courtyard leads to the exit in the far-right corner. The courtyard is lined with pillars rebuilt after the A.D. 62 earthquake. Take a close look at the brick, mortar, and fake-marble stucco veneer.

• *Sneak out of the House of the Faun through its back door and turn right. (If this exit is closed, return to the entrance and make a U-turn left, around to the back of the house.) Thirty yards down, along the right-hand side of the street are metal cages protecting...*

⑫ Original Lead Pipes

These 2,000-year-old pipes (made of lead imported from Britannia) were part of the city's elaborate water system. From the aqueduct-fed water tank at the high end of town, three independent pipe systems supplied water to the city: one for baths, one for private homes, and one for public water fountains. If there was a water shortage, democratic priorities prevailed: First the baths were cut off, then the private homes. The last water supply to go was the public fountains, where all citizens could get drinking and cooking water.

• *If the street's not closed off, take your first left (on Vicolo dei Vettii), walk about 20 yards, and find the entrance (on the left) to the next stop. (If the street—or the house—is closed, turn right instead, and skip down to the next set of directions.)*

⑬ House of the Vettii (Casa dei Vettii)

Pompeii's best-preserved home has been completely blocked off for years; unfortunately, it's unlikely to reopen in time for your visit. The House of the Vettii was the bachelor pad of two wealthy merchant brothers. If you can see the entryway, you may spot the huge erection. This is not pornography. There's a meaning here: The penis and the sack of money balance each other on the goldsmith scale above a fine bowl of fruit. Translation: Only with a balance of fertility and money can you have abundance.

If it's open, step into the atrium with its ceiling open to the sky to collect light and rainwater. The pool, while decorative, was also a functional water-supply tank. It's flanked by large money boxes anchored to the floor. The brothers were certainly successful merchants, and possibly moneylenders, too.

Exit on the right, passing the tight servant quarters, and go into the kitchen, with its bronze cooking pots (and an exposed lead pipe on the back wall). The passage dead-ends in the little Venus Room, which features erotic frescoes behind glass.

Return to the atrium and pass into the big colonnaded garden. It was replanted according to the plan indicated by the traces of roots that were excavated from the volcanic ash. Richly frescoed entertainment rooms ring this courtyard. Circle counterclockwise. The dining room is finely decorated in black and "Pompeiian red" (from iron rust). Study the detail. Notice the lead humidity seal between the wall and the floor, designed to keep the moisture-sensitive frescoes dry. (Had Leonardo da Vinci taken this clever step, his *Last Supper* in Milan might be in better shape today.) Continuing around, you'll see more of the square white stones inlaid in the floor. Imagine them reflecting like cats' eyes as the brothers and their friends wandered around by oil lamp late at night. Frescoes in the Yellow Room (near the exit) show off the ancient mastery of perspective, which would not be matched elsewhere in Europe for nearly 1,500 years.

• *Facing the entrance to the House of the Vettii, turn left and walk downhill one long block (along Vicolo dei Vettii) to a T-intersection (Via della Fortuna), marked by a stone fountain with a bull's head for a spout. Intersections like this were busy neighborhood centers, where the rent was highest and people gathered.*

With the fountain at your back, turn left, then immediately right, walking along a gently curving road (Vicolo Storto). On the left side of the street, at #22, find four big stone cylinders. (If Vicolo Storto is fenced off, continue down the street and take the next possible right, then right again—looping around the closed-off block.)

⑭ Bakery and Mill (Forno e Mulini)

The brick oven looks like a modern-day pizza oven. The stubby stone towers are flour grinders. Grain was poured into the top, and donkeys or slaves pushed wooden bars that turned the stones. The powdered grain dropped out of the bottom as flour—flavored with tiny bits of rock. Each neighborhood had a bakery like this.

Continue to the next intersection (Via degli Augustali, marked *REG VII INS XII*, where there's another fast-food joint, at

#33) and turn left. As you walk, look at the destructive power of all the vines, and notice how deeply the chariot grooves have worn into the pavement. Deep grooves could break wagon wheels. The suddenly ungroovy stretch indicates that this road was in the process of being re-paved when the eruption shut everything down.

• *Head about 50 yards down this (obviously one-way) street to #44 (on the left). Here you'll find the Taberna Hedones (with a small atrium, den, and garden). This bar still has its original floor and, deeper in, the mosaic arch of a grotto fountain. Just past the tavern, turn right and walk downhill to #18, on the right.*

Possible detour: If the road past the tavern is blocked off, here's an-other way to reach the next stop: First, backtrack to the Forum—go back the way you came, turn left at the bull's-head fountain, then turn left again at the aqueduct arch. Back in the Forum, head down to the far end and turn left onto the main street, Via Abbondanza (which we looked down earlier—remember the beaver teeth?). Follow this, turning left up the street after the second fountain (marked REG VII INS I, with a small Vicolo del Lupanare sign). This leads to the entrance of the...

⓮ Brothel (Lupanare)

You'll find the biggest crowds in Pompeii at a place that was likely popular 2,000 ago, too—the brothel. Prostitutes were nicknamed *lupe* (she-wolves), alluding to the call they made when trying to attract business. The brothel was a simple place, with beds and pil-lows made of stone. The ancient graffiti includes tallies and ex-otic names of the women, indicating the prostitutes came from all corners of the Mediterranean (it also served as feedback from satisfied customers). The faded frescoes above the cells may have been a kind of menu for services offered. Note the idealized women (white, which was considered beautiful; one wears an early bra) and the rougher men (dark, considered horny). The bed legs came with little disk-like barriers to keep critters from crawling up.

• *Leaving the brothel, go right, then take the first left, and continue going downhill two blocks to the intersection with Pompeii's main drag, Via Abbondanza. The Forum—and exit—are to the right, for those who may wish to opt out from here.*

The huge amphitheater—which is certainly skippable—is 10 min-utes to your left. But for now, go left for 60 yards, then turn right just beyond the fountain, and walk down Via dei Teatri (labeled REG VIII

INS IV). *Turn left before the columns, and head downhill another 60 yards to #28, which marks the...*

⓰ Temple of Isis

This temple served Pompeii's Egyptian community. The little white stucco shrine with the modern plastic roof housed holy water from the Nile. Isis, from Egyptian myth, was one of many foreign gods adopted by the eclectic Romans. Pompeii must have had a synagogue, too, but it has yet to be excavated.

• *Exit the temple where you entered, and go right. At the next intersection, turn right again, and head downhill to the adjacent theaters. Your goal is the large theater down the corridor at #20, but if it's closed, look at the adjoining, smaller, but similar theater (Teatro Piccolo) just beyond at #19. (Once inside the small theater, you may be able to find a path to the big one.)*

⓱ Theater

Originally a Greek theater (Greeks built theirs with the help of a hillside), this was the birthplace of the Greek port here in 470 B.C.

During Roman times, the theater sat 5,000 people in three sets of seats, all with different prices: the five marble terraces up close (filled with romantic wooden seats for two), the main section, and the cheap nosebleed section (surviving only on the high end, near the trees). The square stones above the cheap seats once supported a canvas rooftop. Take note of the high-profile boxes, flanking the stage, for guests of honor. From this perch, you can see the gladiator barracks—the colonnaded courtyard beyond the theater. They lived in tiny rooms, trained in the courtyard, and fought in the nearby amphitheater.

• *You've seen Pompeii's highlights. When you're ready to leave, backtrack to the main road and turn left, going uphill to the Forum, where you'll find the main exit. For a shortcut back to the entrance area (with the bookstore, luggage storage, and quickest access to the train station), when you are halfway down the exit ramp, take the eight steps on the right and follow the signs. Otherwise, you'll end up on the main road—where you'll head right and loop around.*

    However, there's much more to see—three-quarters of Pompeii's 164 acres have been excavated, but this tour has covered only a third of the site. After the theater—if you still have energy to see more—go back to the main road and take a right toward the eastern part of the site, where the crowds thin out. Go straight for about 10 minutes, likely jogging right after a bit (just follow the posted maps). You'll wind up passing through a pretty, forested area. At the far end is the...

⓲ Amphitheater

If you can, climb to the upper level of the amphitheater (though the stairs are often blocked). With Vesuvius looming in the back-

ground, mentally replace the tourists below with gladiators and wild animals locked in combat. Walk along the top of the amphitheater and look down into the grassy rectangular area surrounded by columns. This is the **Palaestra,** an area once used for athletic training. (If you can't get to the top of the amphitheater, you can see the Palaestra from outside—in fact, you can't miss it, as it's right next door.) Facing the other way, look for the bell tower that tops the roofline of the modern city of Pompei, where locals go about their daily lives in the shadow of the volcano, just as their ancestors did 2,000 years ago.

• *If it's too crowded to bear hiking back along uneven lanes to the entrance, you can slip out the site's "back door," which is next to the amphitheater. Exiting, turn right and follow the site's wall all the way back to the entrance.*

Herculaneum

Smaller, less crowded, and not as ruined as its famous big sister, Herculaneum (worth ▲▲, Ercolano in Italian) offers a closer, more intimate peek into ancient Roman life but lacks the grandeur of Pompeii (there's barely a colonnade).

GETTING THERE

Ercolano Scavi, the nearest train station to Herculaneum, is about 20 minutes from Naples and 50 minutes from Sorrento on the same Circumvesuviana train that goes to Pompeii. Walking from the Ercolano Scavi train station to the ruins takes 10 minutes: Leave the station and turn right, then left down the main drag; continue straight, eight blocks gradually downhill, to the end of the road, where you'll run right into the grand arch that marks the entrance to the ruins. (Skip Museo MAV.) Pass through the arch and continue 200 yards down the path—taking in the bird's-eye first impression of the site to your right—to the ticket office in the modern building.

ORIENTATION TO HERCULANEUM

Cost and Hours: €11, free first Sun of each month, €20 combo-ticket includes Pompeii and three lesser sites (valid 3 consecutive days); also covered by the Campania ArteCard. Open daily April-Oct 8:30-19:30, Nov-March 8:30-17:00, ticket office closes 1.5 hours earlier.

Closures: Like Pompeii, various sections of Herculaneum can be closed unexpectedly. Use this book's map (or the one available on site) to navigate around any closures.

Information: Pick up a free, detailed map and excellent booklet at the info desk next to the ticket window. The booklet gives you a quick explanation of each building. There's a bookstore inside the site, next to the audioguide stand. Tel. 081-777-7008, www.pompeiisites.org.

Tours: The informative and interesting audioguide sheds light on the ruins and life in Herculaneum in the first century A.D. (€6.50, €10/2 people, ID required, rent at kiosk near site entry).

Length of This Tour: Allow one hour.

Baggage Storage: Herculaneum is harder than Pompeii for those with luggage, but not impossible. Herculaneum's train station has lots of stairs and no baggage storage, but you can roll wheeled luggage down to the ruins and store it for free in a locked area in the ticket office building (pick up bags at least 30 minutes prior to site closing). To get back to the station, consider splurging on a €5 taxi (ask the staff to call one for you).

Services: There's a free WC in the ticket office building, and another near the site entry.

Eating: There are vending machines and café tables near the entry to the site. There are also several eateries on the way from the train station.

SELF-GUIDED TOUR

Caked and baked by the same A.D. 79 eruption that pummeled Pompeii, Herculaneum is a small community of intact buildings with plenty of surviving detail. While Pompeii was initially smothered in ash, Herculaneum was spared at first—due to the direction of the wind—but got slammed about 12 hours after the eruption started by a superheated avalanche of ash and hot gases roaring off the volcano. The city was eventually buried under nearly 60 feet of ash, which hardened into tuff, perfectly preserving the city until excavations began in 1748.

After leaving the ticket building, go through the turnstiles and walk the path below the site to the entrance. Look seaward and note where the shoreline is today; before the eruption, it was just where you are standing, a quarter-mile inland. This gives you a sense of just how much volcanic material piled up. The present-day city of Ercolano looms just above the ruins. The modern buildings don't look much different from their ancient counterparts.

As you cross the modern bridge into the excavation site, look down into the moat-like **ditch.** On one side, you see Herculaneum's seafront wall. On the other, the wall that you've just been walking on is the solidified ash layer from the volcano and shows how deeply the town was buried.

After crossing the bridge, stroll straight to the end of the street and find the **College of the Augustali** (Sede degli Augustali, #24). Decorated with frescoes of Hercules (for whom this city was named), it belonged to an association of freed slaves working together to climb their way up the ladder of Roman society. Here and farther on, look around doorways and ceilings to spot ancient wood charred by the pyroclastic flows. Most buildings were made of stone, with wooden floors and beams (which were preserved here by the ash but rarely survive at ancient sites).

Leave the building through the back and go to the right, down the lane. The adjacent *thermopolium* (#19) was the Roman equivalent of a lunch counter or fast-food joint, with giant jars for wine, oil, and snacks. Most of the buildings along here were shops, with apartments above.

A few steps on, the **Bottega ad Cucumas** wine shop (#14, on the right) still has charred remains of beams, and its drink list remains frescoed on the outside wall (under glass).

Take the next right, go halfway down the street, and on the left find the **House of Neptune and Amphitrite** (Casa di Nettuno e Anfitrite, #7). Outside, notice the intact upper floor and imagine it going even higher. Inside, you'll see colorful mosaics and a unique "frame" made of shells.

Back outside, continue downhill to the intersection, then head left for a block and proceed straight across the street into the don't-miss-it **sports complex** (*palestra;* #4). First you'll see a row of "marble" columns, which (look closer) are actually made of rounded bricks covered with a thick layer of plaster, shaped to look

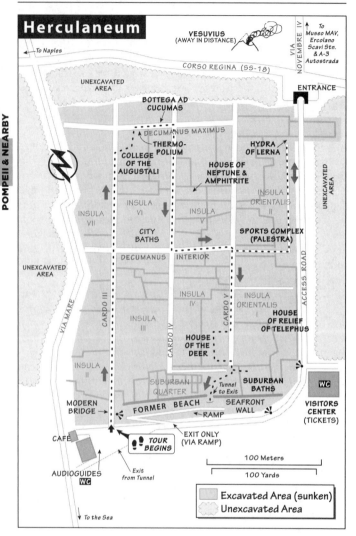

like carved marble. While important buildings in Rome had solid marble columns, these fakes are typical of ordinary buildings.

Continuing deeper into the complex, look for the hole in the hillside and walk through one of the triangular-shaped entrances to find the highlight: the Hydra of Lerna, a sculpted bronze fountain that features the seven-headed monster defeated by Hercules as one of his 12 labors. If this cavernous space is unlit, go to the second doorway on the left wall and press the light switch.

Return through the sports complex and turn downhill to the **House of the Deer** (Casa dei Cervi, #21). It's named for the stat-

ues of deer being attacked by dogs in the garden courtyard (these are copies; the originals are in the Archaeological Museum in Naples). As you wander through the rooms, notice the colorfully frescoed walls. Ancient Herculaneum, like all Roman cities of that age, was filled with color, rather than the stark white we often imagine (even the statues were painted).

You can see more of these colors, this time bright orange, across the street in the **House of Relief of Telephus** (Casa del Rivielo del Telefo, #2).

Continue downhill through the archway. The **Suburban Baths** illustrate the city's devastation (Terme Suburbane, #3; enter near the side of the statue on the terrace, sometimes closed). After you descend into the baths, look back at the steps. You'll see the original wood charred in the disaster, protected by the wooden planks you just walked on. At the bottom of the stairs, in the waiting room to the right, notice where the floor collapsed under the sheer weight of the volcanic debris. (The sunken pavement reveals the baths' heating system: hot air generated by wood-burning furnaces and circulated between the different levels of the floor.) A doorway in front of the stairs is still filled with solidified ash. Despite the damage, elements of refinement remain intact, such as the delicate stuccoes in the *caldarium* (hot bath).

Back outside, make your way down the steps to the sunken area just below. As you descend, you're walking across what was formerly Herculaneum's beach. Looking back, you'll see **arches** that were part of boat storage areas. Archaeologists used to wonder why so few victims were found in Herculaneum. But during excavations in 1981, hundreds of skeletons were discovered here, between the wall of volcanic stone behind you and the city in front of you. Some of Herculaneum's 4,000 citizens tried to escape by sea, but were overtaken by the pyroclastic flows.

Thankfully, your escape is easier. Either follow the sound of water and continue through the tunnel (you'll climb up and pop out near the site entry), or, more scenically, backtrack and exit the same way you entered.

POMPEII & NEARBY

Vesuvius

The 4,000-foot-high Vesuvius, mainland Europe's only active volcano, has been sleeping restlessly since 1944. While Europe has other dangerous volcanoes, only Vesuvius sits in the middle of a three-million-person metropolitan area that would be impossible to evacuate quickly.

Many tourists don't know that you can easily visit the summit. Up top, it's desolate and lunar-like, and the rocks are newly created. Walk the entire accessible part of the crater lip for the most interesting views; the far end overlooks Pompeii. Be still. Listen to the wind and the occasional cascades of rocks tumbling into the crater. Any steam? Vesuvius is closed to visitors when erupting.

You can reach the volcano by bus, taxi, or private car (described below). No matter how you travel up, you'll land at the parking lot. From here it's a steep 30-minute hike (with a 950-foot elevation gain) to the top for a sweeping view of the Bay of Naples. Bring a coat; it's often cold and windy (especially Oct-April).

Cost and Hours: €10 covers entry to the national park (and a mandatory but brief introduction from a park guide, who then sets you free), daily April-Oct 9:30-17:00, until 18:00 in summer, Nov-March 9:30-15:00, these are last entry times—stays open 1.5 hours later, primitive WC only (plan ahead), tel. 081-865-3911 or 081-239-5653, www.vesuviopark.it.

GETTING TO VESUVIUS

By Car or Taxi: Drivers take the exit *Torre del Greco* and follow the signs to *Vesuvio*. Just drive to the end of the road and pay €2.50 to park. A taxi costs €90 round-trip from Naples, including a 2-hour wait; it's about €70 from Pompeii.

By Bus from Pompeii: From the Pompei Scavi train station on the Circumvesuviana line (just outside the main entrance to the Pompeii ruins), you have two bus services to choose from, each taking about three hours (40 minutes up, 40 minutes down, and about 1.5 hours at the summit).

Busvia del Vesuvio winds you up a bumpy private road through the back of the national park in a cross between a shuttle bus and a monster truck. It's a fun, more scenic way to go, but not for the easily queasy. Note that at the top, this bus drops you near the main parking lot—leaving you with a similar uphill walk to the crater (€22 includes summit admission, runs hourly April-

Oct Mon-Sat 9:00-15:00, also at 16:00 and 17:00 June-Aug, rarely runs Sun or Nov-March—call for schedule, buy tickets at "info point" at Pompei Scavi train station, mobile 340-935-2616, www.busviadelvesuvio.com).

The old-fashioned **Vesuvius Trolley Tram** (Tramvia del Vesuvio) uses the main road up (€12 round-trip plus €10 summit admission, 10 percent discount with this book, 6/day, tickets sold at and departs from Camping Zeus next to Pompei Scavi train station, tel. 081-861-5320, www.campingzeus.it).

By Bus from Herculaneum: The quickest trip up is on the **Vesuvio Express.** These small buses leave from the Ercolano Scavi train station (on the Circumvesuviana line, where you get off for the Herculaneum ruins; €10 round-trip plus €10 summit admission, daily from 9:30, runs every 45 minutes based on demand, 20 minutes each way—about 2.5 hours total, office on square in front of train station, tel. 081-739-3666, www.vesuvioexpress.it).

SORRENTO AND CAPRI

Just an hour south of Naples and without a hint of big-city chaos, serene Sorrento makes an ideal home base for exploring this fascinating region, from Naples to the Amalfi Coast to Paestum. And the jet-setting island of Capri is just a short cruise from Sorrento, offering more charm and fun than its glitzy reputation would lead you to believe (at least, outside of the crowded months of July and August).

Sorrento

Wedged on a ledge under the mountains and over the Mediterranean, spritzed by lemon and olive groves, Sorrento is an attractive resort of 20,000 residents and, in summer, just as many tourists. It's as well-located for regional sightseeing as it is a fine place to stay and stroll. The Sorrentines have gone out of their way to create a completely safe and relaxed place for tourists to come and spend money. As 90 percent of the town's economy is tourism, everyone seems to speak fluent English and work for the Chamber of Commerce. This gateway to the Amalfi Coast has an unspoiled old quarter, a lively shopping street, and a spectacular cliffside setting. Residents are proud of the many world-class romantics who've vacationed here, such as famed tenor Enrico Caruso, who chose Sorrento as the place to spend his last weeks in 1921.

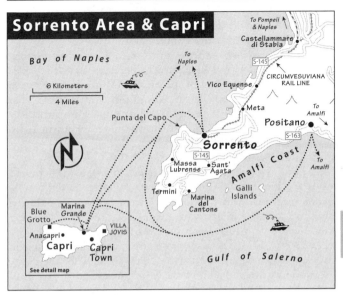

Sorrento Area & Capri

Bay of Naples

6 Kilometers

4 Miles

To Pompeii & Naples

Castellammare di Stabia

To Naples

S-145

CIRCUMVESUVIANA RAIL LINE

Vico Equense

Meta

To Amalfi

Positano

S-163

Punta del Capo

Sorrento

S-145

Massa Lubrense

Sant' Agata

Amalfi Coast

To Amalfi

Termini

Marina del Cantone

Galli Islands

Blue Grotto

Marina Grande

VILLA JOVIS

Anacapri

Capri

Capri Town

See detail map

Gulf of Salerno

PLANNING YOUR TIME

Sorrento itself has no world-class sights, but can easily give you a few pleasant hours. More importantly, Sorrento is a fine base for visiting Naples (by boat or train); Pompeii, Herculaneum, and Mount Vesuvius (by train, plus a bus for Vesuvius); the Amalfi Coast (by bus); and the island of Capri (by boat). All of these destinations are within an hour or so of Sorrento. Of the region's attractions, only Paestum's Greek temples are a little hard to reach from Sorrento, and even they can be seen in a long day.

Sorrento hibernates in winter, and many places close down from November through March.

Orientation to Sorrento

Downtown Sorrento is long and narrow. Piazza Tasso marks the town's center. The congested main drag, Corso Italia, runs paral-

lel to the sea, passing 50 yards below the train station, through Piazza Tasso, and then out toward the cape, where the road's name becomes Via Capo. Nearly everything mentioned here (except Meta beach and the hotels on Via Capo) is within a 10-minute walk of the station. The town is perched on a cliff (some hotels have elevators down to sundecks on the water); the best real beaches are a couple of miles away.

Sorrento has two separate port areas: The Marina Piccola, below Piazza Tasso, is a functional harbor with boats to Naples and Capri, as well as cruise-ship tenders. (While the big cruise ships dock in Naples, smaller ships drop anchor at Sorrento.) The Marina Grande, below the other end of downtown, is a little fishing village, with recommended restaurants and more charm.

TOURIST INFORMATION

The helpful regional TI (labeled *Azienda di Soggiorno*)—located inside the **Foreigners' Club**—hands out the free monthly *Surrentum* magazine, with a great city map and schedules of boats, buses, concerts, and festivals (Mon-Fri 8:30-19:00, Sat-Sun 9:00-13:00 except closed Sun Oct-May; Via Luigi de Maio 35, tel. 081-807-4033, www.sorrentotourism.com; Nino, Fabiola, and Peppe). If you arrive after the TI closes, look for their useful handouts in the lobby of the Foreigners' Club (open until midnight).

You'll also find several small "Info Points" conveniently located around town. These hand out maps and *Surrentum* magazine, and can answer basic questions. You'll find one just outside the **train station** in the green caboose (daily 10:00-13:00 & 15:00-19:00); near **Piazza Tasso** at the corner of Via Correale (under the yellow church, daily 10:00-13:00 & 16:00-21:00); at **Marina Piccola,** where cruise ship tenders and boats from Naples arrive (daily 9:00-17:00, but closed Nov-March); and at the Achille Lauro **parking garage**.

ARRIVAL IN SORRENTO

By Train or Bus: Sorrento is the last stop on the Circumvesuviana train line. In front of the train station is the town's main bus stop, as well as taxis waiting to overcharge you (€15 minimum). All recommended hotels—except those on Via Capo—are within a 10-minute walk.

By Boat: Passenger boats and cruise tenders dock at Marina Piccola. As you walk toward town from the marina, go up the big staircase where the pier bends. Standing on the promenade and facing town, you'll see a TI kiosk and ticket windows for boats to Capri and Naples in the lower area to your left; the bus stop directly ahead; and the elevator up to town to the right, about a five-minute walk along the base of the cliff (€1, follow *lift/acensore* signs). The bus is the easiest option, since it takes you directly to Piazza Tasso in the middle of town. Just catch the next bus (either the city bus, buy ticket before boarding at the nearby ticket window; or the private gray bus, buy ticket on board; either way, the ride costs €1.20

and takes just a few minutes; buses generally depart at least every 20 minutes). If you ride the elevator up to the Villa Comunale city park, exit through the park gate and bear left; Piazza Tasso is about four blocks away.

By Car: The Achille Lauro underground parking garage is centrally located, just a couple of blocks in front of the train station (€2/hour, €24/24 hours, on Via Correale).

HELPFUL HINTS

Church Services: The **cathedral** hosts an English-language Anglican service at 17:00 most Sundays from April to October (but not in August). At **Santa Maria delle Grazie** (perhaps the most beautiful Baroque church in town), cloistered nuns sing from above and out of sight during a Mass each morning at 7:30 (on Via delle Grazie).

Bookstore: Libreria Tasso has a decent selection of books in English, including this one (daily 9:30-23:00, shorter hours Oct-March, Via San Cesareo 96, one block north of cathedral, near Sorrento Men's Club, tel. 081-807-1639).

Laundry: Sorrento has two handy self-service launderettes (about €8/load wash and dry, includes soap; both open daily 7:00-24:00, shorter hours off-season). One launderette is in the old center, just down the alley next to Corso Italia 30 (Vico I Fuoro 3, mobile 338-506-0942). The other is a couple of long blocks past the station, at the corner of Corso Italia and Via degli Aranci.

Guided Tours of Pompeii, Naples, the Amalfi Coast, and the Isle of Capri: Naples-based **Mondo Guide** offers affordable tours of these destinations, including an Amalfi Coast drive that starts from Sorrento. You'll sign up in advance and team up with fellow Rick Steves readers to split the cost.

Local Guides: Giovanna Donadio is a good tour guide for Sorrento, Amalfi, and Capri (€100/half-day, €160/day, same price for any size group, mobile 338-466-0114, giovanna_dona@hotmail.com). **Giovanni Visetti** is a nature lover, mapmaker, and orienteer who organizes hikes and has a fine website describing local trails (mobile 339-694-2911, www.giovis.com, giovis@giovis.com).

GETTING AROUND SORRENTO

By Bus: City buses (usually orange or red-and-white) all stop near the main square, Piazza Tasso, and run until 20:00. Bus #A takes a long route parallel to the coast, heading east to Meta beach or west to the hotels on Via Capo and beyond (about 3/hour); buses #B and #C make a loop up and down, connecting the port (Marina Piccola) to the town center; and bus #D heads to the

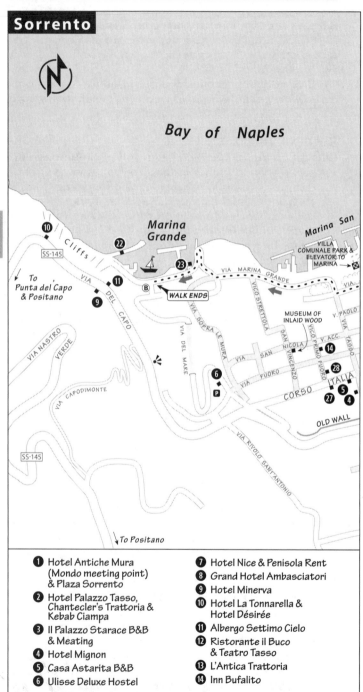

SORRENTO & CAPRI

Sorrento

Bay of Naples

Marina Grande

Marina San

VILLA COMUNALE PARK & ELEVATOR TO MARINA

SS-145

Cliffs

VIA DEL CAPO

To Punta del Capo & Positano

VIA MARINA GRANDE

VIA

WALK ENDS

VICO STRETTOLA

MUSEUM OF INLAID WOOD

V. PAOLO

VIA TASSO

VIA NASTRO VERDE

VIA SOPRA LE MURA

VIA DEL MARE

VIA SAN VINCENZO

SAN NICOLA

VICO PRIMO FIORO

V. ACC.

VIA CAPODIMONTE

VIA FUORO

CORSO ITALIA

OLD WALL

SS-145

VIA RIVOLO SANT'ANTONIO

To Positano

1. Hotel Antiche Mura (Mondo meeting point) & Plaza Sorrento
2. Hotel Palazzo Tasso, Chantecler's Trattoria & Kebab Ciampa
3. Il Palazzo Starace B&B & Meating
4. Hotel Mignon
5. Casa Astarita B&B
6. Ulisse Deluxe Hostel
7. Hotel Nice & Penisola Rent
8. Grand Hotel Ambasciatori
9. Hotel Minerva
10. Hotel La Tonnarella & Hotel Désirée
11. Albergo Settimo Cielo
12. Ristorante il Buco & Teatro Tasso
13. L'Antica Trattoria
14. Inn Bufalito

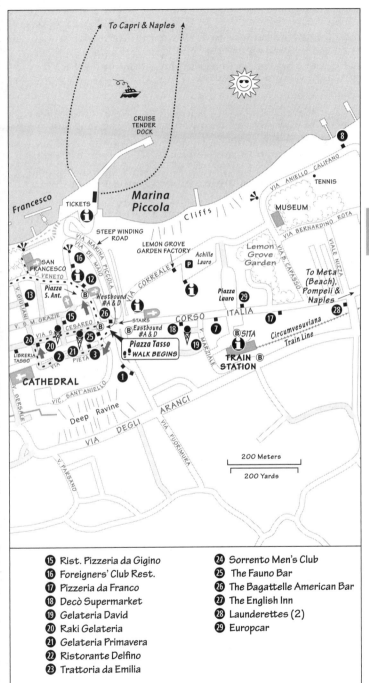

SORRENTO & CAPRI

⑮ Rist. Pizzeria da Gigino
⑯ Foreigners' Club Rest.
⑰ Pizzeria da Franco
⑱ Decò Supermarket
⑲ Gelateria David
⑳ Raki Gelateria
㉑ Gelateria Primavera
㉒ Ristorante Delfino
㉓ Trattoria da Emilia

㉔ Sorrento Men's Club
㉕ The Fauno Bar
㉖ The Bagattelle American Bar
㉗ The English Inn
㉘ Launderettes (2)
㉙ Europcar

fishing village (Marina Grande). The trip between Piazza Tasso and Marina Piccola costs just €1.20; for other trips, tickets cost €1.60 and are good for up to one hour (purchase at tobacco shops and newsstands). Stamp your ticket upon entering the bus. The €8, 24-hour Costiera Sita Sud pass covers Sorrento and the entire Amalfi Coast.

Bus stops can be tricky to find. Buses #A and #D stop where Corso Italia passes through Piazza Tasso. If you're heading west (to Via Capo or Marina Grande), find the stop at the west end of the piazza, across from the statue of Torquato Tasso. If you're heading east (to Meta), catch it in front of the yellow church at the east end of the piazza. Buses #B and #C stop at the corner of Piazza Sant'Antonino, just down the hill toward the water.

A different bus (often gray, operated by a private company) runs only between the port and Piazza Tasso (3/hour in season, €1.20, buy ticket from driver, not covered by 24-hour pass).

By Scooter: Many places rent motor scooters for about €35 per day, including two locations near the train station: **Europcar** (Corso Italia 210p, tel. 081-878-1386, www.sorrento.it) and **Penisola Rent,** in Hotel Nice (Corso Italia 259, tel. 081-877-4664, www.penisolarent.com). Don't rent a vehicle in summer unless you enjoy traffic jams.

By Taxi: Taxis are expensive, charging an outrageous €15 for the short ride from the station to most hotels (more for Via Capo). Because of heavy traffic and the complex one-way road system, you can often walk faster than you can ride. If you do use a taxi, even if you agree to a set price, be sure it has a meter (all official taxis have one). I think taxis are a huge rip-off, since city officials don't have the nerve to regulate them, and hotels are afraid to alienate them. Walk or take the bus instead.

By Bus Tour: To see more of the Sorrentine Peninsula, consider **CitySightseeing Sorrento**'s hop-on, hop-off bus tours, with headphone commentary about the two bays flanking this scenic spit of land (€12, buy tickets on board, daily 4/day April-Oct, full loop is seven stops in 1.75 hours, departs from front of train station, www.sorrento.city-sightseeing.it). The same company's Amalfi Coast bus is a good alternative for linking to Amalfi or Positano if the public buses are too crowded. Skip the pointless **tourist train** you'll see departing from Piazza Tasso, which loops only through the town itself.

Sorrento Walk

Get to know Sorrento with this lazy self-guided town stroll that ends down by the waterside at the small-boat harbor, Marina Grande.

• *Begin on the main square. Stand under the flags with your back to the sea, and face...*

Piazza Tasso

As in any southern Italian town, this "piazza" is Sorrento's living room. It may be noisy and congested, but locals want to be where  the action is...and be part of the scene. The most expensive apartments and top cafés are on or near this square. City buses stop at or close to the square on their way to Marina Piccola and Via Capo. The train station is a five-minute walk to the left. A statue of St. Anthony, patron of Sorrento, faces north as if greeting those coming from Naples (he's often equipped with an armload of fresh lemons and oranges).

This square spans a gorge that divides downtown Sorrento. The newer section (to your left) was farm country just two centuries ago. The older part is to your right, with an ancient Greek gridded street plan (like much of southern Italy, Sorrento was Greek-speaking for centuries before it was Romanized).

For a glimpse at the city's gorge-gouged landscape, consider this quick detour: With the water to your back, cross (carefully) through the square and walk straight ahead a block inland, under a canopy of trees and past a long taxi queue. Belly up to the green railing in front of Hotel Antiche Mure and look down to see steps that were carved in the fifth century B.C. The combination of the gorge and the seaside cliffs made Sorrento easy to defend. A small section of wall closed the landward gap in the city's defenses (you can still see fragments today a few blocks away, near Hotel Mignon).

Sorrento's name may come from the Greek word for "siren," the legendary half-bird, half-woman who sang an intoxicating lullaby. According to Homer, the sirens lived on an island near here. No one had ever sailed by the sirens without succumbing to their incredible musical charms...and to death. But Homer's hero Ulysses was determined to hear the song. He put wax in his oarsmen's ears and had himself lashed to the mast of his ship. Oh, it was nice. The sirens, thinking they had lost their powers, threw themselves into the sea, and the place became safe to inhabit. Ulysses' odyssey was all about the westward expansion of Greek culture, and to the ancient Greeks, places like Sorrento were the wild, wild west.

• *Back at Piazza Tasso, face the sea and head to the far-left corner of the square. You'll find a...*

SORRENTO & CAPRI

Statue of Torquato Tasso

The square's namesake, a Sorrento native, was a lively Renaissance poet—but today he seems only to wonder which restaurant to choose for dinner. Directly behind the statue, pop into the **Fattoria Terranova** shop, one of the zillions of fun, touristy boutiques in Sorrento that sells regional goodies and offers free biscuits and tastes of liqueurs. This one makes all of its own entirely organic products on its own *agriturismo* farm outside the city.

Just to the right of the shop, peek into the big courtyard of **Palazzo Correale** (#18) to get a feel for an 18th-century aristocratic palace's courtyard, its walls lined with characteristic tiles.

• *As you're leaving the courtyard, on your immediate left you'll see the narrow...*

Via Santa Maria della Pietà

Here, just a few yards off the noisy main drag, is a street that goes back centuries before Christ. About 100 yards down the lane, at #24 (on the left), find a 13th-century palace (no balconies back then...for security reasons), now an elementary school. A few steps farther on, you'll see a tiny shrine across the street. Typical of southern Italy, it's where the faithful pray to their saint, who contacts Mary, who contacts Jesus, who contacts God. This shrine is a bit more direct—it starts right with Mary.

• *Continue down the lane, which ends at the delightful...*

Cathedral

Walk alongside this long church until you reach the doors facing the street, halfway down. Step inside the outer door (free, daily 8:00-12:30 & 16:30-20:30, no visits during Mass), and examine the impressive *intarsio* (inlaid-wood) interior doors. They're inlaid on both sides and show scenes of the town and its industry, as well as an old-town map. These were made to celebrate the pope's visit in 1992. Now continue into the church for a cool stroll around the ambulatory, checking out the intricate inlaid Stations of the Cross. Work your way toward the back door. Before exiting, on the right find the fine *presepe* (manger scene). This one takes Bethlehem on that first Christmas and sets it in Naples—with pasta, mozzarella, salami, and even Mount Vesuvius in the background. Exiting through the back door, notice that these doors are also finely inlaid wood.

• *Backtrack 10 yards down Via Santa Maria della Pietà, turn left at the passage under the covered arcade, and cross busy Corso Italia.*

Corso Italia and the Old Town

In the summer, this stretch of road is closed to traffic each evening, when it hosts the best of the *passeggiata*. Look back at the bell tower, with the scavenged ancient Roman columns at its base. Now go straight down Via P. Reginaldo Giuliani, following the old Greek street plan. Locals claim the ancient Greeks laid out the streets east-west for the most sunlight and north-south for the prevailing and cooling breeze. Pause at the poster board on your right to see who's died lately.

• *One block ahead, on your right, the 14th-century loggia is home to the...*

Sorrento Men's Club

Once the meeting place of the town's nobles, this club has been a retreat for retired working-class men for generations. Strictly no women—and no phones.

SORRENTO & CAPRI

Italian men venerate their mothers. (Italians joke that Jesus must have been a southern Italian because his mother believed her son was God, he believed his mom was a virgin, and he lived at home with her until he was 30.) But Italian men have also built into their culture ways to be on their own. Here, men play cards and gossip under an historic emblem of the city and a finely frescoed 16th-century dome, with its marvelous 3-D scenes.

• *Turn right for a better view of the Men's Club and a historical marker describing the building. Then continue along...*

Via San Cesareo

This touristy pedestrian-only shopping street leads back to Piazza Tasso. It's lined with competitive little shops where you can peruse (and sample) lemon products. Notice the huge ancient doorways with their tiny doors—to let the right people in, carefully, during a more dangerous age.

• *After a block, take a left onto Via degli Archi, go under the arch, and then hang a right (under another arch) to the square with the...*

Statue of St. Anthony (Antonino)

Sorrento's town saint humbly looms among the palms, facing the basilica where the reliquary containing a few of his bones lies (free, downstairs in the crypt beneath the altar, surrounded by lots of votives).

• *Exit the square at the bottom-left (following the* Lift to the Port *signs; don't go down the street with the line of trees and the* Porto *signs). Watch on the left for* **The Corner Shop***, where Giovanni sells a wide variety of wines, limoncello, pastas, and other foods, specializing in high-quality* *products from the Campania region. Soon after, on the right you'll see the trees in front of the Imperial Hotel Tramontano, and to their right a path leading to a...*

Cliffside Square

This fine public square, the Villa Comunale, overlooks the harbor. Belly up to the banister to enjoy the view of Marina Piccola and the Bay of Naples. From here, steps zigzag down to the harbor, where lounge chairs, filled by vacationers working on tans, line the sundecks (there's also a €1 elevator to the harbor). The Franciscan church fronting this square faces a fine modern statue of Francis across the street. Next to the church is a dreamy

little cloister. Pop inside to see Sicilian Gothic—a 13th-century mix of Norman, Gothic, and Arabic styles, all around the old pepper tree. This is an understandably popular spot for weddings and concerts.

• From here, you can quit the walk and stay in the town center, or continue another few minutes downhill to the waterfront at Marina Grande (if it's before 20:00, you'll be able to catch a bus back; otherwise, you'll have to walk back uphill). To continue on to Marina Grande, return to the road and keep going downhill. At the next square (Piazza della Vittoria), which offers another grand view, cut over to the road closest to the water. After winding steeply down for a few minutes, it turns into a wide stairway, then makes a sharp and steep switchback (take the right fork to continue downhill). Farther down, just before reaching the waterfront, you pass under an...

Ancient Greek Gate

This gate marks the boundary between Sorrento and Marina Grande, technically a separate town with its own proud residents—it's said that even their cats look different. Because Marina Grande dwellers lived outside the wall and were more susceptible to rape, pillage, and plunder, Sorrentines believe that they come from Saracen (Turkish pirate) stock. Sorrentines still scare their children by saying, "Behave—or the Turks will take you away."

• *Now go all the way down the steps into Marina Grande, Sorrento's "big" small-boat harbor.*

Marina Grande

Until recently, this little community was famously traditional, with its economy based on its fishing fleet. Locals recall when women

wore black when a relative died (1 year for an uncle, aunt, or sibling; 2-3 years for a husband or parent). Men got off easy, just wearing a black memorial button.

There are two recommended restaurants on the harbor. **Trattoria da Emilia** has an old newspaper clipping, tacked near the door, about Sophia Loren filming here. On the far side of the harbor, **Ristorante Delfino** boasts a sundeck for a lazy drink before or after lunch.

• *From here, buses return to the center at Piazza Tasso every hour. Or you can walk back up.*

Sights in Sorrento

▲▲Strolling

Take time to explore the surprisingly pleasant old city between Corso Italia and the sea. Views from Villa Comunale, the public

park next to Imperial Hotel Tramontano, are worth the detour. Each night in summer (May-Oct at 19:30; Nov-April weekends only), the police close off Corso Italia to traffic, and Sorrento's main drag becomes a thriving people scene. The *passeggiata* peaks at about 22:00. (When Piazza Tasso and the main thoroughfare are closed to traffic, buses for Via Capo leave from up on Via degli Aranci, a short walk from Piazza Tasso along Via Fuorimura.)

Lemon Products Galore

Via San Cesareo is lined with hardworking rival shops selling a mind-boggling array of lemon products and offering samples of lots of sour goodies. You'll find *limoncello*, lemon biscuits, lemon pasta, lemon drops, lemon chocolate, lemon perfume, lemon soap, and on and on. Poke around for a pungent experience (and read the "Lemons" sidebar, later). A few produce stands are also mixed in.

▲Lemon Grove Garden (Giardini di Cataldo)

This small park consists of an inviting organic lemon and orange grove lined with shady, welcoming paths. The owners of the grove are seasoned green thumbs, having worked the orchard through many generations. They've even grafted orange-tree branches onto a lemon tree so that both fruits now grow on the same tree. The garden is dotted with benches, tables, and an inviting little tasting (and buying) stand. You'll get a chance to sniff and taste the varieties of lemons, and enjoy free samples of chilled *limoncello* along with other homemade liqueurs made from basil, mandarins, or fennel.

Cost and Hours: Enthusiastically free, daily 10:00-sunset, closed in rainy weather, tel. 081-878-1888, www.igiardinidicataldo.it. Enter the garden either on Corso Italia (100 yards north of the train station—where painted tiles show lemon fantasies) or at the intersection of Via Capasso and Via Rota (next to Hotel La Meridiana Sorrento).

Nearby: The family's small "factory"—where you can see them making these products and buy a tasty gelato, *granita,* or lemonade—is just past the parking garage along the road below the garden (Via Correale 27). They also have a small shop across from the Corso Italia entrance (at #267).

Museum of Inlaid Wood
(Museobottega della Tarsialignea)

Sorrento doesn't have much in the way of museums, but if you want to get out of the heat and crowds, this is a good place to do it. It's not only a collection of inlaid wood, but also a painting gallery featuring scenes of 19th-century Sorrento, antique maps, and portraits, as well as a fine decorative arts collection. The basement displays modern examples of inlaid wood. While pricey, it's serious, thoughtfully presented, and bursting with local pride.

Cost and Hours: €8, daily April-Oct 10:00-18:30, Nov-March 10:00-17:30, Via San Nicola 28, tel. 081-877-1942, www.museomuta.it.

▲Swimming near Sorrento

If you require immediate tanning, you can rent a chair on a pier by the port. There are no great beaches in Sorrento—the gravelly, jam-packed private beaches of **Marina Piccola** are more for partying than pampering, and there's just a tiny spot for public use. The elevator in Villa Comunale city park (next to the Church of San Francesco) gets you down for €1. At **Marina Grande,** Restaurant Delfino has a pier lined with rentable lounge chairs for sunbathing (free for those with this book who buy lunch).

There's a classic, sandy Italian beach two miles away at **Meta,**

Lemons

Around here, *limoni* are ubiquitous: screaming yellow painted on ceramics, dainty bottles of *limoncello*, and lemons the size of softballs at the fruit stand.

The Amalfi Coast and Sorrento area produce several different kinds of lemons. The gigantic, bumpy "lemons" are actually citrons, called *cedri*, and are more for show—they're pulpier than they are juicy, and make a good marmalade. The juicy *sfusato sorrentino*, grown only in Sorrento, is shaped like an American football, while the *sfusato amalfitano*, with knobby points on both ends, is less juicy but equally aromatic. These two kinds of luscious lemons are used in sweets such as *granita* (shaved ice doused in lemonade), *limoncello* (a candy-like liqueur with a big kick, called *limoncino* on the Cinque Terre), *delizia* (a dome of fluffy cake filled and slathered with a thick whipped lemon cream), *spremuta di limone* (fresh-squeezed lemon juice), and, of course, gelato or *sorbetto alla limone*.

although it's generally overrun by teenagers from Naples. While the Meta Circumvesuviana stop is a very long walk from the beach (or a €25 cab ride), bus #A goes directly from Piazza Tasso to Meta beach (last stop, schedule posted for hourly returns). At Meta, you'll find pizzerias, snack bars, and a little free section of beach, but the place is mostly dominated by several sprawling private-beach complexes—if you go, pay for a spot in one of these. Lido Metamare seems best (May-Sept; lockable changing cabins, lounge chairs, and more available for an extra fee; tel. 081-532-2505). It's a very Italian scene—locals complain that it's "too local" (i.e., inundated with riffraff)—with light lunches, a playground, a manicured beach, loud pop music...and no international tourists.

Tarzan might take Jane to the wild and stony beach at **Punta del Capo,** a 15-minute bus ride from Piazza Tasso (the same bus #A explained above, but in the opposite direction from Meta; 2/hour, get off at stop in front of the American Bar, then walk 10 minutes past ruined Roman Villa di Pollio).

Another good choice is **Marina di Puolo,** a tiny fishing town popular in the summer for its sandy beach, surfside restaurants, and beachfront disco (to get here, stay on bus #A a bit farther—ask driver to let you off at Marina di Puolo—then follow signs and hike down about 15 minutes).

More Activities

The Sorrento Sport Snack Bar has two **tennis courts** open to the public (long hours daily, pay to use the court and rent equipment, call to reserve, across from recommended Grand Hotel Ambasciatori at Via Califano 5, tel. 081-807-1616).

To escape the shops, go **snorkeling** or **scuba diving** in the Mediterranean. Contact Futuro Mare for details on the one-hour boat ride out to the protected marine zone that lies between Sorrento and Capri (options for snorkelers, beginners, and experienced certified divers; about 3 hours round-trip, call 1-2 days in advance to reserve, tel. 349-653-6323, www.sorrentodiving.it, info@futuromare.it).

You can **rent motorboats** big enough for four people (with your back to the ferry-ticket offices, it's to the left around the corner at Via Marina Piccola 43; tel. 081-807-2283, www.nauticasicsic.com).

Nightlife in Sorrento

PUBS AND CLUBS

Sorrento is a fun place to enjoy a drink or some dancing after dinner. The crowd is older, and the many local English expats seem to have paved the way for you.

The Fauno Bar, which dominates Piazza Tasso with tables spilling onto the square, is a fine place to make the scene over a drink any time of day.

The Bagattelle American Bar, run by DJ Daniele, who tailors music to the audience (including karaoke if you ask nicely), is the oldest club in town. The scene, while sloppy, is generally comfortable for the 30- to 60-year-old crowd. If you're alone, there's a pole you can dance with (no cover charge, €4-7 drinks—including their signature cocktail, "Come Back to Sorrento," a mojito made with *limoncello*—no food, nightly from 21:30, down the steps from the flags at Piazza Tasso).

The English Inn offers both a streetside pub and a more refined-feeling garden out back—at least until the evening, when the music starts blaring. English vacationers come to Sorrento in droves (many have holidayed here annually for decades). The menu includes fish-and-chips, all-day English breakfast, baked beans on toast, and draft beer (daily, Corso Italia 55, tel. 081-878-2570).

The Foreigners' Club offers live Neapolitan songs, Sinatra-style classics, and jazzy elevator music nightly at 20:00 throughout the summer. It's just right for old-timers feeling frisky (in the center).

THEATER SHOW

At **Teatro Tasso,** a hardworking troupe puts on *The Sorrento Musical,* a folk-music show that treats visitors to a schmaltzy dose of Neapolitan Tarantella music and dance—complete with "Funiculì Funiculà" and "Santa Loo-chee-yee-yah." The 75-minute Italian-language extravaganza features a cast of 14 playing guitar, mandolin, saxophone, and tambourines, and singing operatically from Neapolitan balconies...complete with Vesuvius erupting in the background. Your €25 ticket (€50 with 4-course dinner) includes a drink before and after the show. Maurizio promises my readers a €5 discount if you buy directly from the box office and show this book (maximum 2 tickets per book, 3-5 nights/week mid-April-Oct at 21:30, bar opens 30 minutes before show, dinner starts at 20:00 and must be reserved in advance—in person or by email, box office open virtually all day long, theater seats 500, facing Piazza Sant'Antonino in the old town, tel. 081-807-5525, www. teatrotasso.com, info@teatrotasso.com).

Sleeping in Sorrento

Given the location, hotels here often have beautiful views, and many offer balconies. At hotels that offer sea views, ask for a room *"con balcone, con vista sul mare"* (with a balcony, with a sea view). *"Tranquillo"* is taken as a request for a quieter room off the street.

Hotels listed are either near the train station and city center (where balconies overlook city streets) or on cliffside Via Capo (with sea-view balconies). Via Capo is a 20-minute walk—or short bus ride—from the station.

You should have no trouble finding a room any time except in August, when the town is jammed with Italians and prices often rise above the regular high-season rates quoted here. Rates are soft in April and October, and tend to drop by about a third from November to March at the hotels that don't close for the winter. Always contact hotels directly, mention this book, and ask for their best rate.

Note: The spindly, more exotic, and more tranquil Amalfi Coast town of Positano (see next chapter) is also a good place to spend the night.

IN THE TOWN CENTER

$$$ Hotel Antiche Mura, with 50 rooms and four stars, is sophisticated, elegant, and plush. It offers all the amenities you could need, including an impressive breakfast buffet. Surrounded by lemon trees, the pool and sundeck offer a peaceful oasis. Just a block off the main square, it's quieter than some central hotels because it's perched on the ledge of a dramatic ravine (small-windowed Db-

---

Sleep Code

Abbreviations   (€1=about $1.10, country code: 39)
S=Single, **D**=Double/Twin, **T**=Triple, **Q**=Quad, **b**=bathroom
Price Rankings
  $$$ **Higher Priced**—Most rooms €140 or more
   $$ **Moderately Priced**—Most rooms €85-140
    $ **Lower Priced**—Most rooms €85 or less

Unless otherwise noted, credit cards are accepted, breakfast is included, free Wi-Fi and/or a guest computer is generally available, and English is spoken. Many towns in Italy levy a hotel tax of €1.50-5 per person, per night (often collected in cash; usually not included in the rates I've quoted). Prices change; verify current rates online or by email. For the best prices, always book directly with the hotel.

€150, regular Db-€219, balcony Db-€279, Tb-€299, Qb-€340; Michele promises 15 percent off prevailing rates in 2016 if you reserve directly with the hotel, mention this book, and pay cash; air-con, elevator, parking-€10/day, a block inland from Piazza Tasso at Via Fuorimura 7, tel. 081-807-3523, www.hotelantichemura.com, info@hotelantichemura.com).

$$$ Hotel Palazzo Tasso, nicely located near the center, has 11 small, sleek, modern rooms, though there's very little public space and peak season prices are high (rates change by the day, Db-up to €220 in peak season, "deluxe" room with balcony-€20 extra, air-con, elevator, Via Santa Maria della Pietà 33, tel. 081-878-3579, www.palazzotasso.com, info@palazzotasso.com).

$$$ Plaza Sorrento is a contemporary-feeling, upscale refuge in the very center of town (next door to Antiche Mura, but not as elegant). Its 65 rooms mix mod decor with wood grain, and the rooftop swimming pool is inviting. Their "comfort" and "superior" rooms offer balconies for €20-40 more (standard Db-€180, Tb-€230, 10 percent discount if you reserve directly with hotel and show this book, elevator, air-con, Via Fuorimura 3, tel. 081-877-1056, www.plazasorrento.com, info@plazasorrento.com).

$$ Il Palazzo Starace B&B, conscientiously run by Massimo, offers seven tidy, modern rooms in a little alley off Corso Italia, one block from Piazza Tasso (Db-€120-130 depending on size, balcony-€15 extra, five-bed family room-€170, 10 percent off with cash and this book in 2016, air-con, lots of stairs, no elevator but a luggage dumbwaiter, ring bell around corner from Via Santa Maria della Pietà 9, tel. 081-807-2633, mobile 366-950-5377, www.palazzostarace.com, info@palazzostarace.com).

$$ Hotel Mignon rents 22 soothing blue rooms with beautiful, tiled public spaces, a rooftop sundeck, and a small garden surrounded by a lemon grove (Sb-€80, Db-€120-€130, Tb-€150, these prices good with this book when you reserve directly with the hotel, air-con, most rooms have balconies but no views; from the cathedral, walk a block farther up Corso Italia and look for the hotel up a small gated lane to your left; Via Sersale 9, tel. 081-807-3824, www.sorrentohotelmignon.com, info@sorrentohotelmignon.com, Paolo).

$$ Casa Astarita B&B, hiding upstairs in a big building facing the busy main street, has a crazy-quilt-tiled entryway and six bright, tranquil, air-conditioned rooms (three with little balconies). Thin doors, echoey tile, and a buzzing location can result in noise... bring earplugs (Db-€120, Tb-€140, book direct for best price, air-con, 50 yards past the cathedral on Corso Italia at #67, tel. 081-877-4906, www.casastarita.com, info@casastarita.com, Annamaria and Alfonso). If there's no one at reception, ask at Hotel Mignon (described above)—the same family runs both hotels.

$ Ulisse Deluxe Hostel is the best budget deal in town. This "hostel" is actually a hotel, with 56 well-equipped, marble-tiled rooms and elegant public areas, but it also has two six-bed dorm rooms (hotel: Db-€80, Tb-€120, Qb-€160; hostel: €25/bunk in single-sex dorm; breakfast buffet-€10, these rates valid when you mention this book and reserve directly, air-con, elevator, spa and pool use extra, parking-€10/day, Via del Mare 22, tel. 081-877-4753, www.ulissedeluxe.com, info@ulissedeluxe.com, Chiara). The hostel is a five-minute walk from the old-town action: From Corso Italia, walk down the stairs just beyond the hospital *(ospedale)* to Via del Mare. Go downhill along the right side of the big parking lot to find the entrance.

$ Hotel Nice rents 29 simple, cramped, cheap rooms with high ceilings 100 yards in front of the train station on the noisy main drag. This last resort is worth considering only for its very handy-to-the-train-station location. Alfonso promises that you can have a quiet room—critical given the thin windows and busy location—if you request it with your booking email (Sb-€50, €60 in Aug; Db-€75, €90 in Aug; extra bed-€25; 10 percent discount when you book direct with the hotel, mention this book, and pay cash; air-con, elevator, rooftop terrace, closed Nov-March, Corso Italia 257, tel. 081-878-1650, www.hotelnice.it, info@hotelnice.it).

AT THE EAST END OF TOWN

$$$ Grand Hotel Ambasciatori is a sumptuous four-star hotel with 100 rooms, a cliffside setting, a sprawling garden, and a pool. This is Humphrey Bogart land, with plush public spaces, a relaxing stay-awhile ambience, and a free elevator to its "private beach"— actually a sundeck built out over the water (prices vary wildly, but in high season generally: viewless Db-€200, sea-view Db-€350, 10 percent discount with this book if you book directly with the hotel, website specials, elevator, air-con in summer, balconies in most rooms, parking-€21/day, closed Nov-March, Via Califano 18, tel. 081-878-2025, www.ambasciatorisorrento.com, ambasciatori@manniellohotels.com). It's a short walk beyond the town center (10-15 minutes from the train station or Piazza Tasso). To reach it, go a block in front of the train station, turn right onto Corso Italia, then left down Via Capasso (which eventually winds right and becomes Via Califano).

WITH A VIEW, ON VIA CAPO

These cliffside hotels are outside of town, toward the cape of the peninsula (from the train station, go straight out Corso Italia, which turns into Via Capo). Once you're set up, commuting into town by bus or on foot is easy. Hotel Minerva is my favorite Sorrento splurge, while Hotel Désirée is a super budget bet with comparable views. If you're in Sorrento to stay put and luxuriate, especially with a car, these accommodations are perfect (although I'd rather luxuriate in Positano—see next chapter).

Getting to Via Capo: From the city center, it's a gradually uphill 15-minute walk (20 minutes from train station, last part is a bit steeper), a €20 taxi ride, or a cheap bus ride. If you're arriving with luggage, you can wait at the train station for one of the long-distance SITA buses (usually red or green-and-white) that stop on Via Capo on their way to Massa Lubrense (about every 40 minutes; some buses heading for Positano/Amalfi also work—check with the driver). Frequent Sorrento city buses leave from Piazza Tasso in the city center, a five-minute walk from the station (go down a block and turn left on Corso Italia; from far side of the piazza, look for bus #A, about 3/hour). Tickets for either bus are sold at the station newsstand and tobacco shops (€1.60). Get off at the Hotel Belair stop for the hotels listed here. If you're headed to Via Capo after 19:30 or on Sunday, when the center can be closed to traffic (including the Piazza Tasso bus stop), catch the bus instead on Via degli Aranci (with your back to the station, wind left, up and around it; the bus stop is near Bar Paradise).

Getting from Via Capo into Town: Buses work great once you get the hang of them (and it's particularly gratifying to avoid the taxi racket). To reach downtown Sorrento from Via Capo, catch any bus heading downhill from Hotel Belair (3/hour, buses run all day and evening).

$$$ Hotel Minerva is like a sun-worshipper's temple. The road-level entrance (on a busy street) leads to an elevator that takes you to the fifth-floor reception. Getting off, you'll step onto a spectacular terrace with outrageous Mediterranean views. Bright common areas, a small rooftop swimming pool, and a cold-water Jacuzzi complement 60 large, tiled, colorful rooms with views, some with balconies (Db-€170, Tb-€210, balcony-€20 extra, these discounted prices promised through 2016 if you reserve directly with the hotel and mention this book, 3-night peak season minimum, air-con, parking-€15/day, closed Nov-March, Via Capo 30, tel. 081-878-1011, www.minervasorrento.com, info@minervasorrento. com).

$$$ Hotel La Tonnarella is an old-time Sorrentine villa turned boutique hotel, with several terraces, stylish tiles, and indifferent service. Eighteen of its 24 rooms have views of the sea (nonview Db-€155, "superior" sea-view or balcony Db-€200, "deluxe" Db with view terrace-€220, exotic view suite with terrace-€330, email or check website for best rates, extra bed-€50, air-con, parking-€5/day, small beach with private elevator access, closed Nov-March, Via Capo 31, tel. 081-878-1153, www.latonnarella.it, info@latonnarella.it).

$$ Albergo Settimo Cielo ("Seventh Heaven") is an old-fashioned, family-run cliff-hanger sitting 300 steps above Marina Grande. The reception is just off the waterfront side of the road, and the elevator passes down through four floors with 50 clean but spartan rooms—all with grand views, and many with balconies. The rooms feel dated for the price—you're paying for the views (Db-€140, Tb-€180, Qb-€215, slightly cheaper without balcony, check website for specials, mention this book for 5 percent discount on these rates when reserving directly with hotel, air-con in summer, free parking with this book, inviting pool, sun terrace, closed Nov-March, Via Capo 27, tel. 081-878-1012, www. hotelsettimocielo.com, info@hotelsettimocielo.com; Giuseppe, sons Stefano and Massimo, and daughter Serena).

$$ Hotel Désirée is a modest affair, with reasonable rates, humbler vistas, and no traffic noise. The 22 basic rooms have high, ravine-facing or partial-sea views, and half come with balconies (all the same price). There's a fine rooftop sunning terrace and a lovable cat, Tia. Owner Corinna (a committed environmentalist), daughter Cassandra, and receptionist Antonio serve an organic breakfast and are hugely helpful with tips on exploring the peninsula (Sb-€64, small Db-€79, Db-€89, Tb-€109, Qb-€119, most rooms have fans, lots of stairs with no elevator, laundry-€8, free parking, shares driveway and beach elevator with La Tonnarella, closed early-Nov-Feb except for Christmas—rare for this area, Via Capo 31, tel. 081-878-1563, www.desireehotelsorrento.com, info@ desireehotelsorrento.com).

Eating in Sorrento

GOURMET SPLURGES DOWNTOWN

In a town proud to have no McDonald's, consider eating well for a few extra bucks. Both of these places are worthwhile splurges run by a hands-on boss with a passion for good food and exacting service. The first is gourmet and playful. The second is classic. Both are romantic. Be prepared to relax and stay awhile.

Ristorante il Buco, once the cellar of an old monastery, is now a small, dressy restaurant that serves delightfully presented, playful, and creative modern Mediterranean dishes under a grand, rustic arch. Peppe and his staff love to explain exactly what's on the plate. The dashing team of cooks builds sophisticated dishes with an emphasis on seafood in a state-of-the-art kitchen. Peppe holds a Michelin star and designs his menu around whatever's fresh. Reservations are often necessary to dine inside under their elegant vault (€20-24 pastas, €25-28 *secondi,* dinners run from about €50 plus wine, extravagant tasting *menu*s for €75-100, 10 percent discount when you show this book, good vegetarian selection, Thu-Tue 12:30-14:30 & 19:30-23:00, closed Wed and Jan; just off Piazza Sant'Antonino—facing the basilica, go under the grand arch on the left and immediately enter the restaurant at II Rampa Marina Piccola 5; tel. 081-878-2354, www.ilbucoristorante.it).

L'Antica Trattoria enjoys a sedate, *romantico,* candlelit ambience, tucked away in its own little world. The cuisine is traditional, but with modern flair, and the inviting menu is fun to peruse (though pricey). Run by the same family since 1930, the restaurant has a trellised garden outside and intimate nooks inside. Walk around the labyrinthine interior before you select a place to sit. Aldo and sons will take care of you while Vincenzo—the Joe Cocker-esque resident mandolin player—entertains. They offer several fixed-price meals (including a €20 three-course lunch and a €44 four-course dinner), or you can order à la carte (€20-23 pastas, €30-35 *secondi*). Readers who show this book can choose either a 10 percent discount on one of the fixed-price meals, or a free *limoncello* if you order à la carte. Reservations are smart (good vegetarian options, daily 12:00-23:30, closed Mon Nov-Feb, air-con, Via Padre R. Giuliani 33, tel. 081-807-1082).

MIDPRICED RESTAURANTS DOWNTOWN

Inn Bufalito specializes in all things buffalo: *mozzarella di bufala* (and other buffalo milk cheeses), steak, sausage, salami, carpaccio, and buffalo-meat pasta sauce. The smartly designed space has a modern, borderline-trendy, casual atmosphere and a fun indoor-outdoor vibe (€7-10 salads, €10-13 pastas, €12-18 *secondi,* don't miss the seasonal specialties on the blackboard, daily 12:00-23:00, closed Nov-March, Vico I Fuoro 21, tel. 081-365-6975).

Chantecler's Trattoria is a hole-in-the-wall, family-run place on the narrow lane that leads to the cathedral. Their lunch menu is very affordable: €4 *primi* and €5 *secondi*. At dinner, prices are slightly higher, but still easy on the budget (€6-9 pastas, €9-12 *secondi*, good vegetarian dishes, take out or eat in, Tue-Sun 12:00-15:00 & 18:30-23:00, closed Mon, Via Santa Maria della Pietà 38, tel. 081-807-5868; Luigi, Francesco, and family).

Ristorante Pizzeria da Gigino, lively and congested with a sprawling interior and tables spilling onto the street, makes huge, tasty Neapolitan-style pizzas in their wood-burning oven (€8-12 pizzas and pastas—good gnocchi, €10-15 *secondi*, daily 12:00-24:00, closed Jan-Feb, just off Piazza Sant'Antonino at Via degli Archi 15, tel. 081-878-1927, Antonino).

Meating, as its name implies, focuses on top-quality meats, from homemade sausages to giant steaks on a charcoal grill. They also have vegetarian options and a short, thoughtfully selected list of pastas (€10-20 meals, Wed-Mon 12:00-15:00 & 18:00-24:00, closed Tue, Via Santa Maria della Pietà 20, tel. 081-878-2891).

With a Sea View: The **Foreigners' Club Restaurant** has some of the best sea views in town (with a sprawling terrace under breezy palms), live music nightly at 20:00 (May-mid-Oct), and affordable—if uninspired—meals. It's a good spot for dessert or an after-dinner *limoncello* (€9-14 pastas and pizzas, €13-23 *secondi*, cheaper "snack" menu with €6-8 light meals, daily, bar opens at 9:30, meals served 11:00-23:00, Via Luigi de Maio 35, tel. 081-877-3263). If you'd enjoy eating along the water (rather than just with a water view), see "Harborside in Marina Grande," later.

CHEAP EATS DOWNTOWN

Pizza: **Pizzeria da Franco** seems to be Sorrento's favorite place for basic, casual pizza in a fun, untouristy atmosphere. There's nothing fancy about this place—just locals on benches eating hot sandwiches and great pizzas served on waxed paper in a square tin. It's packed to the rafters with a youthful crowd that doesn't mind the plastic cups (€5-8 pizzas, calzones, sandwiches, and salads, takeout possible, daily 8:00-late, just across from Lemon Grove Garden on busy Corso Italia at #265, tel. 081-877-2066).

Kebabs: **Kebab Ciampa,** a little hole-in-the-wall, has a passionate following among eaters who appreciate Andrea's fresh bread, homemade sauces, and ethic of buying meat fresh each day (and closing when the supply is gone). This is your best non-Italian €6 meal in town. Choose beef or chicken—locals don't go for pork—and garnish with fries and/or salad (nightly from 17:00, before the cathedral off Via Santa Maria della Pietà, at Vico il Traversa Pietà 23, tel. 081-807-4595).

Picnics: Get groceries at the **Decò supermarket** (Mon-Sat 8:30-20:30, Sun 9:30-13:00 & 16:30-20:00, Corso Italia 223).

Gelato: Near the train station, **Gelateria David** has many repeat customers (so many flavors, so little time; they make 145 different flavors, but have about 30 at any one time). In 1957, Augusto Davide opened a *gelateria* in Sorrento, and his grandson Mario proudly carries on the tradition today, still making the gelato on-site. Before choosing a flavor, sample *Profumi di Sorrento* (an explosive sorbet of mixed fruits), "Sorrento moon" (white almond with lemon zest), or lemon crème (daily 9:00-24:00, shorter hours in spring and fall, closed Dec-Feb, a block below the train station at Via Marziale 19, tel. 081-807-3649). Mario also offers gelato-making classes for a behind-the-scenes look at Italy's favorite dessert (€12/person, 5-person minimum, 1 hour, call or email ahead to reserve, gelateriadavid@yahoo.it). Don't mistake this place for the similarly named Gelateria Davide, in the town center.

Raki, conveniently located along the main shopping street in the old center, uses top-notch ingredients and serves some of the creamiest, most flavorful gelato in town (daily 10:30-23:00, closed Jan-Feb, Via San Cesareo 48, mobile 329-877-7922).

At **Gelateria Primavera,** Antonio and Alberta whip up 70 exotic flavors—and still have time to make pastries for the pope and other celebrities...check out the photos. Famous and a bit overrated, it's a Sorrento institution (daily 9:00-24:00, just west of Piazza Tasso at Corso Italia 142, tel. 081-807-3252).

HARBORSIDE IN MARINA GRANDE

For a decent dinner *con vista,* head down to either of these restaurants by Sorrento's small-boat harbor, Marina Grande. To get to Marina Grande, follow the directions from the cliffside square on my self-guided Sorrento walk, earlier. For a less scenic route, walk down Via del Mare, past the recommended Ulisse Deluxe Hostel, to the harbor. Either way, it's about a 15-minute stroll from downtown. You can also take bus #D from Piazza Tasso. Be prepared to walk back (last bus leaves at 20:00) or spring for a pricey taxi.

Ristorante Delfino serves fish in big portions to hungry locals in a quiet and bright, Seattle-style pier restaurant. The cooking, service, and setting are all top-notch. The restaurant is lovingly run by Luisa, her brothers Andrea and Roberto, and her husband Antonio. Show this book for a free glass of *limoncello* to cap the meal. If you're here for lunch, take advantage of the sundeck—show this book to get an hour of relaxation and digestion on the lounge chairs (€12-18 pastas, €18-30 *secondi,* daily 12:00-15:00 & 18:30-22:30, closed Nov-March; at Marina Grande, facing the water, go all the way to the left and follow signs; tel. 081-878-2038).

Trattoria da Emilia, at the opposite end of the tranquil Marina Grande waterfront, is considerably more rustic, less expensive, and good for straightforward, typical Sorrentine home-cooking, including fresh fish, lots of fried seafood, and *gnocchi di mamma*— potato dumplings with meat sauce, basil, and mozzarella (€6-13 pastas, €11-16 *secondi,* daily 12:15-15:00 & 19:00-22:30 except closed Tue Sept-Oct, closed Nov-Feb, no reservations taken, indoor and outdoor seating, tel. 081-807-2720).

Sorrento Connections

It's impressively fast to zip by boat from Sorrento to many coastal towns and islands during the summer—in fact, it's quicker and easier for residents to get around by fast boat than by car or train.

BY TRAIN AND BUS
From Sorrento to Naples, Pompeii, and Herculaneum by Circumvesuviana Train: This commuter train runs twice hourly between Naples and Sorrento (www.eavcampania.it). The schedule is printed in the free *Surrentum* magazine (available at TI). From Sorrento, it's about 30 minutes to Pompeii (€2.20), 50 minutes to Herculaneum (€2.70), and 70 minutes to Naples (€3.60). If there's a line at the train station, you can also buy tickets at the Snack Bar (across from the main ticket office) or downstairs at the newsstand. Note that the risk of theft on this train is mostly limited to suburban Naples. Going between Sorrento and Pompeii or Herculaneum is generally safer.

From Sorrento to Naples Airport: Six Curreri buses run daily to and from the airport (€10, pay driver, daily at 6:30, 8:30, 10:30, 12:00, 14:00, and 16:30, likely 2 additional departures in summer, 1.5 hours, departs from in front of train station, tel. 081-801-5420, www.curreriviaggi.it).

From Sorrento to Rome: Most people ride the Circumvesuviana 70 minutes to Naples, then catch the Frecciarossa or Italo express train to Rome. However, the Sorrento-Rome bus is direct, cheaper, and all on one ticket—although the departure times can be inconvenient. Buses leave Sorrento's train station and arrive at Rome's Tiburtina station (Mon-Sat at 6:00 and 17:00, Sun at 17:00, off-season at 6:00 only, 4 hours; buy tickets at www.marozzivt.it— in Italian only, at some travel agencies, or on board for a surcharge; tel. 080-579-0111).

BY BOAT

The number of boats that run per day varies: The frequency indicated here is for roughly mid-May through mid-October, with more boats per day in the peak of summer and fewer off-season. The specific companies operating each route also tend to change from season to season. Check all schedules locally with the TI, your hotel, or online (use the individual boat company websites—see below—or visit www.capritourism.com, select English, and click on "Shipping timetable"). The Caremar line, a subsidized state-run ferry company, takes cars, offers fewer departures, and is just a bit slower—but cheaper—than the hydrofoil. All of the boats take several hundred people each—and frequently fill up. Boat tickets are sold only at the port; you can buy them for the next day, but only in the evening.

From Sorrento to Capri: Boats run at least hourly. Your options include a fast **ferry** (*traghetto* or *nave veloce*, 4/day, 25 minutes, Caremar, tel. 081-807-3077, www.caremar.it) or a slightly faster, pricier **hydrofoil** (*aliscafi*, up to 20/day, 20 minutes, Gescab, tel. 081-807-1812, www.gescab.it). To visit Capri when it's least crowded, it's best to buy your ticket at 8:00 and take the 8:30 hydrofoil (if you miss it, try to depart by 9:45 at the very latest). These early boats can be jammed, but it's worth it once you reach the island.

From Sorrento to Other Points: Naples (6/day, more in summer, departs roughly every 2 hours starting at 7:20, 35 minutes, NLG), **Positano** (mid-April-mid-Oct only, 2-4/day, 35 minutes, Alicost), **Amalfi** (mid-April-mid-Oct only, 2-4/day, 1 hour, Alicost and Caremar). *Note:* Boats from Sorrento to Positano and Amalfi may not be running; if they aren't, change boats in Capri to reach Amalfi Coast destinations. Ask at the TI for guidance.

Getting to Sorrento's Port (Marina Piccola): To walk, either hike steeply down directly from Piazza Tasso (find the stairs under the flags), or walk to the Villa Comunale public park (see my self-guided Sorrento Walk, earlier), where you can pay €1 to ride the elevator down (from the bottom, it's a 5-minute walk to the port). Otherwise, catch bus #B or #C from Piazza Sant'Antonino (buy ticket at tobacco shop and specify that you're going to the *porto*), or hop on the little gray private bus that leaves from under the flags in Piazza Tasso (pay driver; both buses cost €1.20 and run 3/hour).

Capri

Capri was made famous as the vacation hideaway of Roman emperors Augustus and Tiberius. In the 19th century, it was the haunt

of Romantic Age aristocrats on their Grand Tour of Europe. Later it was briefly a refuge for Europe's artsy gay community: Oscar Wilde, D. H. Lawrence, and company hung out here back when being gay could land you in jail...or worse. And these days, the island is a world-class tourist trap, packed with gawky, nametag-wearing visitors searching for the rich and famous—and finding only their prices.

The "Island of Dreams" is a zoo in July and August—overrun with tacky, low-grade group tourism at its worst. At other times of year, though still crowded, it can provide a relaxing and scenic break from the cultural gauntlet of Italy. Pack your patience, be ready to wait around a bit (for buses, boats, etc.), and try to enjoy being on vacation. What gets lost in all of the fame and glitz is simply how gorgeous a place it is: Chalky white limestone cliffs rocket boldly from the shimmering blue and green surf. Strategically positioned gardens, villas, and other viewpoints provide stunning vistas of the Sorrento Peninsula, Amalfi Coast, Vesuvius, and Capri itself.

PLANNING YOUR TIME

This is the best see-everything-in-a-day plan from Naples or Sorrento: Take an early hydrofoil to Capri (from Sorrento, buy ticket at 8:00, boat leaves around 8:30 and arrives around 8:50—smart). Go directly by boat to the Blue Grotto. Instead of taking the boat back, catch a bus from the grotto to Anacapri, which has two or three hours' worth of sightseeing. In Anacapri, see the town, ride the chairlift to Monte Solaro and back (or hike down), stroll out from the base of the chairlift to Villa San Michele for the view, and eat lunch. Afterward, catch a bus to Capri town, which is worth at least a half-hour. Finally, ride the funicular from Capri town down to the harbor and laze on the free beach or wander the yacht harbor while waiting for your boat back to Sorrento.

If you're heading to Capri specifically to see the Blue Grotto, be sure to check the weather and sea conditions. If the tide is too high or the water too rough, the grotto can be closed. Ask the TI or your hotelier before going.

Efficient travelers can see Capri on the way between destina-

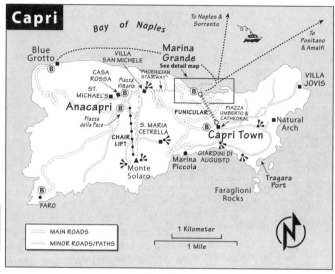

tions: Sail from Sorrento, check your bag at the harbor, see Capri, and take a boat directly from there to Naples or to the Amalfi Coast (or vice versa).

If you buy a one-way ticket to Capri (there's no round-trip discount anyway), you'll have maximum schedule flexibility and can take any convenient hydrofoil or ferry back. (Check times for the last return crossing upon arrival with any TI on Capri, or at www. capritourism.com; the last return trips usually leave between 18:30 and 19:30.) During July and August, however, it's wise to get a round-trip boat ticket with a late return time (ensuring you a spot on a boat at the time they're most crowded)—you can always use the ticket to return earlier if you like. On busy days, be 20 minutes early for the boat, or you can be bumped.

Starting your day as early as is reasonably possible is key to an enjoyable trip to Capri. Day-trippers come down from as far as Rome, creating a daily rush hour in each direction (arriving between 10:00-11:00, leaving around 17:00). If you arrive before them, the entire trip to and into the Blue Grotto might take just a half-hour; arrive later and you might face as much as a two-hour delay.

GETTING TO CAPRI

For instructions on getting to Capri by **public boat,** check the "Connections" sections of the Sorrento and Naples chapters.

Another option is to visit Capri by **tour boat. Mondo Guide** offers my readers a great-value, no-stress, all-day itinerary for €80: You'll be picked up at your Sorrento hotel around 8:00 and driven to the port, where you'll board a small boat (maximum 10 people, shared with other Rick Steves readers) and be taken across to Capri to visit the Blue Grotto (unless it's closed for bad weather; optional €13 entry fee to hop in one of the little rowboats to go in). Then you'll continue to Marina Grande for about four hours of free time on the island—just enough to head to Anacapri for sightseeing and the Monte Solaro chairlift (island transportation and admissions on your own). Finally you'll reboard the boat for a lightly narrated circle around the island and pass through the iconic Faraglioni Rocks (includes drinks, a snack, and—conditions permitting—a chance to swim from the boat). Considering the expense and hassle of doing all of this on your own, the tour is a good value—you're basically paying about €20-30 extra for a less stressful, more personal experience. The trip only goes if enough people sign up, and reservations are required—book online at www.mondoguide.com. If Mondo's tour isn't running on a day that you want to go, **Tempio Travel**—based at the Sorrento train station—offers a very similar trip at a similar price (tel. 081-878-2103, www.tempiotravel.com, or drop by their office).

Orientation to Capri

First thing—pronounce it right: Italians say KAH-pree, not kah-PREE like the song or the pants. The island is small—just four miles by two miles—and is separated from the Sorrentine Peninsula by a narrow strait. Home to 13,000 people, Capri has only two towns to speak of: Capri and Anacapri. The island also has some scant Roman ruins and a few interesting churches and villas. But its chief attraction is its famous Blue Grotto, and its best activity is the chairlift from Anacapri up the island's Monte Solaro.

TOURIST INFORMATION

Capri's efficient English-speaking TI has branches in Marina Grande, Capri town, and Anacapri. Their well-organized website has schedules and practical information in English (www.capritourism.com). At any TI, pick up the free map or pay for a better one if you'll be venturing to the outskirts of Capri town or Anacapri.

The **Marina Grande TI** is by the Motoscafisti Capri tour boat dock (May-Sept Mon-Sat 9:00-13:00 & 15:00-18:15, Sun 9:00-13:00, shorter hours off-season, tel. 081-837-0634).

The **Capri town TI** fills a closet under the bell tower on Piazza Umberto and is less crowded than its sister at the port (same hours as Marina Grande TI, WC and baggage storage downstairs behind TI, tel. 081-837-0686).

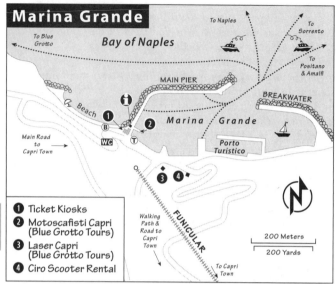

The tiny **Anacapri TI** is on the main pedestrian/shopping street, Via Orlandi, at #59 (Mon-Sat 9:00-15:00, closed Sun, shorter hours Nov-Easter, tel. 081-837-1524).

ARRIVAL IN CAPRI

Approaching Capri: Get oriented on the boat before you dock, as you near the harbor with the island spread out before you. The port is a small community of its own, called **Marina Grande,** connected by a funicular and buses to the rest of the island. **Capri town** fills the ridge high above the harbor. The ruins of Emperor Tiberius' palace, **Villa Jovis,** cap the peak on the left. To the right, the dramatic *"Mamma mia!"* road arcs around the highest mountain on the island **(Monte Solaro),** leading up to **Anacapri** (the island's second town, just out of sight). Notice the old zigzag steps below that road. Until 1874, this was the only connection between Capri and Anacapri. (Though it's quite old, it's nowhere near as old as implied by its nickname, "The Phoenician Stairway.") The white house on the ridge above the zigzags is **Villa San Michele** (where you can go later for a grand view of boats like the one you're on now).

Arrival at Marina Grande: Upon arrival, get your bearings. Find the base of the **funicular railway** (signed *funicolare*) that runs up to Capri town, and stand facing it, with your back to the water.

The fourth little clothing-and-souvenir shop to the right of the funicular provides **baggage storage** (look inside for *left luggage* sign on far back wall, daily 9:00-18:00, tel. 081-837-4575). If it's closed, your best option is at the upper funicular station in Capri town (bag storage near public WCs, daily 7:00-20:00; be aware that you may have to pay extra to take big bags up the funicular).

To your right is a stand of ticket windows with counters for **funicular and bus tickets** and for **boat tickets** to Naples and Sorrento. Just beyond these is the **stop for buses** to the rest of the island. (Notice how long the line is for your destination, and how small the buses are—and line up accordingly.) Across the street is a pay **WC**, and a little farther on is Marina Grande's pebbly public beach.

Two competing companies offer **boat trips** around the island and to the Blue Grotto: Laser Capri and Motoscafisti Capri. You'll see Motoscafisti Capri's ticket shed along the pier; Laser Capri's office is halfway down the waterfront to the left at Via Cristoforo Colombo 69. Both offer similar services (see "Getting Around Capri," later).

The **TI** is along the pier, facing the Motoscafisti Capri dock.

From the port, you can take a boat to the Blue Grotto (my recommended plan) or around the island, the funicular to Capri town, or a bus to various destinations on Capri. If you have energy to burn, you can follow the steep paved footpath that connects the port area with Capri town. It starts a block inland from the ferry dock (follow the signs to *Capri centro;* allow 30 minutes).

HELPFUL HINTS

Cheap Tricks: A cheap day trip to Capri is tough. Hydrofoils from Sorrento cost €17 each way, and a Blue Grotto ticket (plus boat transportation) comes to €32—so you're already pushing €50 per person before you even factor in bus tickets and admissions elsewhere on the island. You can save a few euros by taking the slightly slower (but less frequent) Caremar ferry to Capri instead of the hydrofoil, and another few euros by using the bus to the Blue Grotto instead of the boat. After the boats stop running, anyone willing to swim the few yards in from the little dock can see the Blue Grotto for free (albeit illegally).

Best Real Hike: Serious hikers love the peaceful and scenic three-hour Fortress Hike, which takes you entirely away from the tourists. You'll walk under ruined forts along the rugged coast, from the Blue Grotto to the *faro* (lighthouse). From there, you can take a bus back to Anacapri (3/hour). The TI has a fine map/brochure.

Free Beach: Marina Grande has a free pebbly beach (you can pay for a shower at the bar).

Local Guides: Friendly **Anna Bilardi Leva** lives on Capri and is licensed to guide both on the island and elsewhere around the region (€140/half-day, €200/day, 10 percent discount if you show this book, mobile 339-712-7416, www. capritourinformation.com, annaleva@hotmail.it).

GETTING AROUND CAPRI

By Bus and Funicular: Tickets for the island's buses and funicular cost €1.80 per ride and are available at newsstands, tobacco shops, official ticket offices, or from the driver. Validate your ticket when you board. The €9.60 all-day pass (available only at official ticket offices) barely pays for itself on a short visit.

Schedules are clearly posted at all bus stations. Public buses are orange, while the gray and blue buses are for private tour groups. Public buses from the port to Capri town, and from Capri town to Anacapri, are frequent (4/hour, 10 minutes). The direct bus between the port and Anacapri runs less often (2/hour, 25 minutes). From Anacapri, branch bus lines run to the parking lot above the Blue Grotto and to the Faro lighthouse (3/hour each). Buses are teeny (because of the island's narrow roads) and often packed. At most stops, you'll see ranks for passengers to line up in. When the driver changes the bus's display to read *completo* (full), you just have to wait for the next one.

By Taxi: Taxis have fixed rates (Marina Grande to Capri town-€15; Marina Grande to Anacapri-€20 for 3 people, €2/additional person). You can hire a taxi for about €70 per hour—negotiate.

By Scooter: If you are experienced at riding a scooter, this is the perfect way to have the run of the island. (For novice riders, Capri's steep and narrow roads aren't a good place to start.) **Ciro** proudly rents bright-yellow scooters with 50cc engines—strong enough to haul couples. Rental includes a map and instructions with parking tips and other helpful information (€15/hour, €55/day, €5 discount with this book for 2 hours or more in 2016; includes helmet, gas, and insurance; daily April-Oct 9:30-19:00, may open in good weather off-season, look for Ferrari logo at Via Don Giobbe Ruocco 55, Marina Grande, mobile 338-360-6918, www. capriscooter.com).

Boat Trips Around the Island: Both **Laser Capri** and **Motoscafisti Capri** run quick one-hour trips that circle the island, passing stunning cliffs, caves, and views that most miss when they go only to the Blue Grotto (€18; see contact info under "Blue Grotto," later). With both companies, you can combine the boat trip with a stop at the Blue Grotto at no extra charge (this adds about an hour; check schedules to find out which tours include the optional Blue Grotto stop). As the trip just to the grotto already costs €14, the island circle is well worth the extra €4 (boats leave daily from 9:00 until 13:00 or possibly later—whenever Blue Grotto rowboats stop running).

Sights in Capri

CAPRI TOWN

This is a cute but extremely clogged and touristy shopping town. It's worth a brief visit, including the Giardini di Augusto, before

moving on to more interesting parts of the island.

The funicular drops you just around the corner from Piazza Umberto, the town's main square. With your back to the funicular, the bus stop is 50 yards straight ahead down Via Roma. You'll find the **TI** under the bell tower on Piazza Umberto (see "Tourist Information," earlier). The footpath to the port starts just behind the TI, near the baggage storage (follow signs to *Il Porto,* 15-minute walk).

Capri town's multidomed Baroque **cathedral,** which faces the square, is worth a quick look. Its multicolored marble floor at the altar was scavenged from Emperor Tiberius' villa in the 19th century.

To the left of City Hall (Municipio, lowest corner), a narrow, atmospheric lane leads into the medieval part of town, which has plenty of eateries and is the starting point for the walk to Villa Jovis.

The lane to the left of the cathedral (past Bar Tiberio, under the wide arch) is a fashionable shopping strip that's justifiably been dubbed "**Rodeo Drive**" by residents. Walk a few minutes down Rodeo Drive (past Gelateria Buonocore at #35, with its tempting fresh waffle cones) to Quisisana Hotel, the island's top old-time hotel. From there, head left for fancy shops and villas, and right for gardens and views.

Downhill and to the right, a five-minute walk leads to a lovely public garden, **Giardini di Augusto** (€1, April-Oct daily 9:00-19:30, May and early Nov daily 9:00-17:30, shorter hours and free to enter off-season, no picnicking). While the garden itself is modest, it boasts great views over the famous Faraglioni Rocks—handy if you don't have the time, money, or interest to access the higher vantage points near Anacapri (Monte Solaro, Villa San Michele).

VILLA JOVIS AND THE EMPEROR'S CAPRI

Even before becoming emperor, Augustus loved Capri so much that he traded the family-owned Isle of Ischia to the (then-independent) Neapolitans in exchange for making Capri his personal property. Emperor Tiberius spent a decade here, A.D. 26-37. (Some figure he did so in order to escape being assassinated in Rome.)

Emperor Tiberius' ruined villa, Villa Jovis, is a scenic 45-minute hike from Capri town. You won't find any statues or mosaics here—just an evocative, ruined complex of terraces clinging to a rocky perch over a sheer drop to the sea...and a lovely view. You can make out a large water reservoir for baths, the foundations of servants' quarters, and Tiberius' private apartments (fragments of marble flooring still survive). The ruined lighthouse dates from the Middle Ages.

Cost and Hours: €2, April-Oct Wed-Mon 10:00-18:00, closed Tue, shorter hours and possibly closed off-season—check at Capri TI.

▲▲BLUE GROTTO

Three thousand tourists a day spend a couple of hours visiting Capri's Blue Grotto (Grotta Azzurra). I did—early (when the light is best), without the frustration of crowds, and with choppy waves nearly making entrance impossible...and it was great.

The actual cave experience isn't much: a five-minute dinghy ride through a three-foot-high entry hole to reach a 60-yard-long cave, where the sun reflects brilliantly blue on its limestone bottom. But the experience—getting there, getting in, and getting back—is a scenic hoot. You get a fast ride and scant narration on a 30-foot boat partway around the gorgeous island; along the way, you see bird life and dramatic limestone cliffs. You'll understand why Roman emperors appreciated the invulnerability of the island—it's surrounded by cliffs, with only one good access point, and therefore easy to defend.

Just outside the grotto, your boat idles as you pile into eight-foot dinghies that hold up to four passengers each. Next, you'll be taken to a floating ticket counter and asked to pass the €13 grotto entry fee over the side. From there, your ruffian rower will elbow his way to the tiny hole, then pull fast and hard on the cable at the low point of the swells to squeeze you into the grotto (keep your head down and hands in the boat). Then your man rows you around, spouting off a few descriptive lines and singing "O Sole Mio." Depending upon the strength of the sunshine that day, the blue light inside can be brilliant.

The grotto was actually an ancient Roman *nymphaeum*—a retreat for romantic hanky-panky. Many believe that, in its day, a tunnel led here directly from the palace, and that the grotto experience was enlivened by statues of Poseidon and company, placed half-underwater as if emerging from the sea. It was ancient Romans who smoothed out the entry hole that's still used to this day.

When dropping you off, your boatman will fish for a tip—this is optional, and €1 is enough (you've already paid plenty). If you don't want to return by boat, ask your boatman to let you off at the little dock, where stairs lead up to a café and the Blue Grotto bus stop.

Cost: The €13 entry fee (separate from the €14 ride from Marina Grande) includes €9 for the rowboat service plus €4 to cover the admission to the grotto itself. Though signs forbid it, some people dive in for free from the little dock next to the grotto entrance after the boats stop running—a magical experience and a favorite among locals.

Timing: When waves or high tide make entering dangerous, the boats don't go in—the grotto can close without notice, sending tourists (flush with anticipation) home without a chance to squeeze through the little hole. (If this happens to you, consider the one-hour boat ride around the island instead.)

If you're coming from Capri's port (Marina Grande), allow 1-3 hours for the entire visit, depending on the chaos at the caves. Going with the first trip will get you there at the same time as the boatmen in their dinghies—who hitch a ride behind your boat—resulting in less chaos and a shorter wait at the entry point.

If you arrive on the island later in the morning—when the Blue Grotto is already jammed—you could try waiting to visit until about 15:00, when most of the tour groups have vacated. But this may only work by bus (not boat). Confirm that day's closing time with a TI before making the trip.

Getting There: You can either take the boat directly from Marina Grande, as most people do, or save money by taking the bus via Anacapri.

By Boat from Marina Grande: Two companies make the boat trip from different parts of Marina Grande—Laser Capri and Motoscafisti Capri (€14 round-trip with either company, no one-way discount; Motoscafisti Capri—tel. 081-837-7714, www.motoscafisticapri.com; Laser Capri—tel. 081-837-5208, www.lasercapri.com). The first boats depart Marina Grande at 9:00, and they continue at least until 13:00—or often later, depending on when the rowboats stop running (likely 17:00 in summer, but earlier off-season).

By Bus via Anacapri: If you're on a budget, you can take the bus from Anacapri to the grotto (rather than a boat from Marina Grande). You'll save almost €7, lose time, and see a beautiful, calmer side of the island.

Anacapri-Blue Grotto buses (roughly 3/hour, 10 minutes) depart only from the Anacapri bus station at Piazza della Pace (not from the bus stop at Piazza Vittoria 200 yards away, which is more popular with tourists). If you're coming from Marina Grande or Capri town and want to transfer to the Blue Grotto buses, don't get off when the driver announces "Anacapri." Instead, ride one more stop to Piazza della Pace. If in doubt, ask the driver or a local. At the Piazza della Pace bus station, notice the two lines: Grotta Azzurra for the Blue Grotto, and Faro for the lighthouse.

Getting Back from the Blue Grotto: You can either take the boat back, or ask your boatman to drop you off on the small dock next to the grotto entrance, from where you climb up the stairs to the stop for the bus to Anacapri (if you came by boat, you'll still have to pay the full round-trip boat fare).

ANACAPRI

Capri's second town has two or three hours' worth of interesting sights. Though Anacapri sits higher up on the island ("ana" means "upper" in Greek), there are no sea views at street level in the town center.

When visiting Anacapri by bus, note that there are two stops: Piazza Vittoria, in the center of town near the base of the Monte Solaro chairlift; and 200 yards farther along at Piazza della Pace (pronounced "PAH-chay"), a larger bus station near the cemetery. Piazza Vittoria gets you a bit closer to the main sights (chairlift and Villa San Michele), while Piazza della Pace is where you transfer to the Blue Grotto bus. When leaving Anacapri for Capri town or Marina Grande, buses can be packed. Your best chance of getting a seat is to catch the bus from Piazza della Pace.

Regardless of where you get off, make your way to **Via Orlandi,** Anacapri's pedestrianized main street. From Piazza Vittoria, the street is right there—just go down the lane to the right of the Anacapri statue. From Piazza della Pace, reach it via the crosswalk and then the small lane called Via Filietto. Anacapri's **TI** is at Via Orlandi 59, near Piazza Vittoria.

To see the town, stroll along Via Orlandi for 10 minutes or so. Signs suggest a quick circuit that links the Casa Rossa, St. Michael's Church, and peaceful side streets. You'll also find shops and eateries, including good choices for quick, inexpensive pizza, *panini*, and other goodies (both open daily in peak season): **Sciué Sciué** (same price for informal seating or takeaway, near the TI at #73, tel. 081-837-2068) and **Pizza e Pasta** (takeaway only, just before the church at #157, tel. 328-623-8460).

Of the sights below, the first two are in the heart of town (on or near Via Orlandi), while the next two are a short walk away.

SORRENTO & CAPRI

Casa Rossa (Red House)

This "Pompeiian-red," eccentric home, a hodgepodge of architectural styles, is the former residence of John Clay MacKowen, a Louisiana doctor and ex-Confederate officer who moved to Capri in the 1870s and married a local girl. (MacKowen and the Villa San Michele's Axel Munthe—see later—loathed each other, and even tried to challenge each other to a duel.) Its small collection of 19th-century paintings of scenes from around the island recalls a time before mass tourism. Don't miss the second floor, with more paintings and four ancient, sea-worn statues, which were recovered from the depths of the Blue Grotto in the 1960s and 1970s.

Cost and Hours: €3.50; discounted to €1 with ticket stub from Blue Grotto, Villa San Michele, or Monte Solaro chairlift; June-Sept Tue-Sun 10:00-13:30 & 17:30-20:00; shorter hours April-May and Oct; closed Nov-March and Mon year-round, Via Orlandi 78, tel. 081-838-2193.

▲Church of San Michele

This Baroque church in the village center has a remarkable majolica floor showing paradise on earth in a classic 18th-century Neapoli-

tan style. The entire floor is ornately tiled, featuring an angel (with flaming sword) driving Adam and Eve from paradise. The devil is wrapped around the trunk of a beautiful tree. The animals—happily ignoring this momentous event—all have human expressions. For the best view, climb the spiral stairs from the postcard desk. Services are held only during the first two weeks of Advent, when the church is closed to visitors.

Cost and Hours: €2, daily April-Oct 9:00-18:30, Nov and mid-Dec-March 10:00-14:00, closed late Nov-mid Dec, in town center just off Via Orlandi—look for signs for *San Michele,* tel. 081-837-2396, www.chiesa-san-michele.com.

▲Villa San Michele

This is the 19th-century mansion of Axel Munthe, Capri's grand personality, an idealistic Swedish doctor who lived here until 1943 and whose services to the Swedish royal family brought him into contact with high society. At the very least, walk the path from Piazza Vic-

toria past the villa to a superb, free viewpoint over Capri town, Marina Grande, and—in the distance—Mount Vesuvius and Sorrento. Paying to enter the villa lets you see a few rooms with period furnishings; a well-done but ho-hum exhibit on Munthe; and one of this region's most delightful gardens, with a chapel, Olivetum (a tiny museum of native birds and bugs), and a view that's slightly better than the free one outside. Throughout the gardens and the house, you'll see a smattering of original ancient objects unearthed here—and lots and lots of copies. A café (also with a view) serves affordable sandwiches.

Cost and Hours: €7, May-Sept daily 9:00-18:00, closes earlier Oct-April, tel. 081-837-1401, www.villasanmichele.eu.

Getting There: From Piazza Vittoria, walk up the grand staircase and turn left onto Via Capodimonte. At the start of the shopping street, on your right, pass the deluxe Capri Palace Hotel—venture in if you can get past the treacherously eye-catching swimming pool windows (behind the pillars). After lots of overpriced shops, just before the villa, notice the Swedish Embassy: In honor of Munthe, Swedes get into the villa for free.

▲▲Chairlift up to Monte Solaro

From Anacapri, ride the chairlift *(seggiovia)* to the 1,900-foot summit of Monte Solaro for a commanding view of the Bay of Naples.

Work on your tan as you float over hazelnut, walnut, chestnut, apricot, peach, kiwi, and fig trees, past a montage of tourists (mostly from cruise ships; when the grotto is closed—as it often is—they bring passengers here instead). Prospective smoochers should know that the lift seats are all single. As you ascend, consider how Capri's real estate has been priced out of the locals' reach. The ride takes 13 minutes each way, and you'll want at least 30 minutes on top, where there are picnic benches and a café with WCs.

Cost and Hours: €7.50 one-way, €10 round-trip, daily June-Oct 9:30-17:00, last run down at 17:30, closes earlier Nov-May, confirm schedule with TI, tel. 081-837-1438, www.capriseggiovia.it.

Getting There: From the Piazza Vittoria bus stop, just climb the steps and look right.

At the Summit: You'll enjoy the best panorama possible: lush cliffs busy with seagulls enjoying the ideal nesting spot. Find the Faraglioni Rocks—with tour boats squeezing through every few

minutes—which are an icon
of the island. The pink building nearest the rocks was an
American R&R base during
World War II. Eisenhower
and Churchill met here. On
the peak closest to Cape Sorrento, you can see the distant

ruins of Emperor Tiberius' palace, Villa Jovis. Pipes from the Sorrento Peninsula bring water to Capri (demand for fresh water here
long ago exceeded the supply provided by the island's three natural
springs). The Galli Islands mark the Amalfi Coast in the distance.
Cross the bar terrace for views of Mount Vesuvius and Naples.

Hiking Down: A highlight for hardy walkers (provided you
have strong knees and good shoes) is the 40-minute downhill hike
from the top of Monte Solaro, through lush vegetation and ever-
changing views, past the 14th-century Chapel of Santa Maria Cetrella (at the trail's only intersection, it's a 10-minute detour to the
right), and back into Anacapri. The trail starts downstairs, past the
WCs (last chance). Down two more flights of stairs, look for the
sign to *Anacapri e Cetrella*—you're on your way. While the trail
is well-established, you'll encounter plenty of uneven steps, loose
rocks, and few signs.

Near Anacapri: Faro

The lighthouse, at the rocky, arid, and desolate southwestern corner
of the island, is a favorite place to enjoy the sunset. This area has a
private beach, pool, small restaurants, and a few fishermen. Reach it
by bus from Anacapri (3/hour, departs from Piazza della Pace stop).

Capri Connections

From Capri's Marina Grande by Boat to: Sorrento (fast ferry:
4/day, 25 minutes, Caremar; hydrofoil: up to 20/day, 20 minutes,
Gescab), **Naples** (roughly 2/hour, hydrofoil: 45 minutes; ferries:
60-80 minutes), **Positano** (mid-April-mid-Oct, 2-4/day, 30-60
minutes; less off-season, Gescab), **Amalfi** (mid-April-mid-Oct, 1/
day, 1.5 hours). Confirm the schedule carefully at TIs or www.
capritourism.com—last boats usually leave between 18:00 and
20:10.

AMALFI COAST AND PAESTUM

With its stunning scenery, hill- and harbor-hugging towns, and historic ruins, Amalfi is Italy's coast with the most. The trip from Sorrento to Salerno along the breathtaking Amalfi Coast is one of the world's great bus rides. It will leave your mouth open and your camera's memory card full. You'll gain respect for the 19th-century Italian engineers who built the roads—and even more respect for the 21st-century bus drivers who squeeze past each other here daily. Cantilevered garages, hotels, and villas cling to the vertical terrain, and beautiful sandy coves tease from far below and out of reach. As you hyperventilate, notice how the Mediterranean, a sheer 500-foot drop below, really twinkles. All this beautiful scenery apparently inspires local Romeos and Juliets, with the latex evidence of late-night romantic encounters littering the roadside turnouts. Over the centuries, the spectacular scenery and climate have been a siren call for the rich and famous, luring Roman Emperor Tiberius, Richard Wagner, Sophia Loren, Gore Vidal, and others to the Amalfi Coast's special brand of *la dolce vita*.

Amalfi Coast towns are pretty, but they're also touristy, congested, and overpriced. (For that reason, many visitors prefer side-tripping in from Sorrento.) Most beaches here are private—and pebbly—and access is expensive. Check and understand your bills in this greedy region.

PLANNING YOUR TIME

On a quick visit, use Sorrento (see previous chapter) as your home base and do the Amalfi Coast as a day trip. But for a small-town

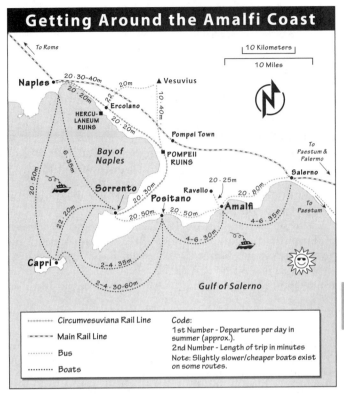

Getting Around the Amalfi Coast

To Rome

10 Kilometers

10 Miles

Naples

20 · 30-40m

20m

Vesuvius

20 · 20m

Ercolano

HERCU-
LANEUM
RUINS

20 · 20m

Pompei Town

Bay of
Naples

POMPEII
RUINS

To
Paestum &
Palermo

Salerno

6 · 35m

20 · 50m

Sorrento

20 · 30m

Positano

Ravello

20 · 25m

20 · 80m

To
Paestum

Amalfi

22 · 20m

20 · 50m

20 · 50m

4-6 · 35m

4-6 · 30m

Capri

2-4 · 35m

2-4 · 30-60m

Gulf of Salerno

Circumvesuviana Rail Line

Main Rail Line

Bus

Boats

Code:
1st Number - Departures per day in
summer (approx.).
2nd Number - Length of trip in minutes
Note: Slightly slower/cheaper boats exist
on some routes.

AMALFI COAST

vacation from your vacation, spend a few more days on the coast,
sleeping in Positano or Amalfi town.

Trying to decide between staying in Sorrento, Positano, or
Amalfi? Sorrento is the largest of the three, with useful services
and the best transportation connections and accommodations. Tiny
Positano is the most chic and picturesque, with a decent beach, but
it's perhaps the most touristy. The town of Amalfi feels like a real,
workaday city—with the most actual sights and good hiking op-
portunities—but it lacks the romantic charm of the others.

GETTING AROUND THE AMALFI COAST

The real thrill here is the scenic Amalfi drive. This is treacherous
stuff—even if you have a car, you may want to take the bus or hire
a driver. Brave souls enjoy seeing the coast by scooter or motorbike
(rent in Sorrento). The most logical springboard for this trip is Sorrento, but Positano and Amalfi work, too.

Below, I've outlined your options by bus, boat, and taxi. Many
travelers do the Amalfi Coast as a round-trip by bus, but a good
strategy is to go one way by bus and return by boat. For example,

instead of bussing from Sorrento to Salerno (end of the line) and back again, consider taking the bus along the coast to Positano and/or Amalfi, then catching the ferry back. Ferries run less often in spring and fall, and some don't run at all off-season (mid-Oct-mid-April). Boats don't run in stormy weather at any time of year. If boats aren't running between Amalfi and Sorrento, change boats in Capri.

Looking for exercise? Consider an Amalfi Coast hike. Numerous trails connect the main coastal towns with villages on the hills. Get a good map before you venture out.

Moving on from the Amalfi Coast: It can be easier to continue around the coast to Salerno, a major transportation hub, rather than retracing your steps to Sorrento. For example, if you're overnighting in Positano or Amalfi and headed to Naples or Rome in the morning, you can catch a boat or bus to Salerno and take advantage of faster trains from there.

By Bus

From Sorrento: SITA buses depart from in front of Sorrento's train station nearly hourly (in peak season, 20/day, marked *Amalfi via Positano*) and stop at all Amalfi Coast towns (Positano in 50 minutes; Amalfi in another 50 minutes). To reach Ravello (the hill town beyond Amalfi) or Salerno (at the far end of the coast), you'll transfer in Amalfi. Ticket prices vary with trip length (one-way to Positano-€1.80, to Amalfi-€2.70; for Ravello, you'll change in Amalfi and pay an extra €1.20). All rides are covered by the 24-hour Costiera SITA Sud pass (€8).

In summer, buses run from 6:30 to 22:00 (they stop running earlier off-season; check schedules). Buy tickets at the tobacco shop or newsstand nearest any bus stop before boarding. At the Sorrento train station, you can buy tickets at the newsstand at street level—labeled *Ticket Point* (daily 7:00-20:00, closed 13:30-14:30 off-season, also sells Circumvesuviana train tickets). Tickets are also sold at the less reliable info booth outside near the bus stop. If both are closed, try the appropriately named Snack Bar, upstairs in the station; or Bar Frisby, just down the hill.

Line up under the *Bus Stop SITA* sign across from the train station (10 steps down). A schedule is posted on the wall: Carefully note the lettered codes that differentiate daily buses from weekend-only buses. *Giornaliero (G)* means daily; *Feriale (F)* denotes Monday-Saturday departures; and *Festivo (H)* is for Sundays and holidays. After 19:30 and on Sundays (check sign at

AMALFI COAST

main bus stop), the main Corso Italia through town may be closed to traffic; if so, buses may leave from Via degli Aranci (with your back to the station, go left and wind around it; the bus stop is near Bar Paradise).

Leaving Sorrento, grab a seat on the right for the best views. If you return by bus, it's fun to sit directly behind the driver for a box seat with a view over the twisting hairpin action. Sitting toward the front will also help minimize carsickness.

Avoiding Crowded Buses: Amalfi Coast buses are routinely unable to handle the demand during summer months and holidays. Generally, if you don't get on one bus, you're well-positioned to catch the next one (bring a book). Try to arrive early in the morning. Remember that buses start running as early as 6:30; beginning at 8:30, they leave about every 30 minutes. Departures between 9:00 and 11:00 are crowded and frustrating. Count the number of people in line: Buses pull into Sorrento empty and seat 48 (plus 25 standing). Note that an eight-seater minibus and driver costs about €300 for the day—if you can organize a small group, €40 per person is a very good deal. (For options, see "By Taxi," later.)

Returning to Sorrento: Summer congestion can be so bad—particularly in July and August—that return buses don't even stop in Positano (because they filled up in Amalfi). Those trying to get back to Sorrento are stuck with taking an extortionist taxi or, if in Positano, hopping a boat...if one's running. If touring the coast by bus, do Positano first and come home from Amalfi to avoid the problem of full buses.

Alternative Private Bus: From April through October, **City-Sightseeing Sorrento**'s bright red buses travel between Sorrento, Positano, and Amalfi, offering commentary along the way. They're more expensive than the public bus, but worth considering if the public buses are full (regardless of your destination, first leg is €10, and each subsequent leg is €6; buy tickets onboard, departs hourly from Sorrento's train station starting at 8:45, www.sorrento. city-sightseeing.it).

By Boat

Boats stop at Sorrento, Positano, Amalfi, and Salerno, generally from mid-April through mid-October. Check schedules carefully: Routes vary by season and may be suspended without notice (few boats run off-season). The specific companies operating each route change frequently, compete for passengers, and usually claim to know nothing about their rivals' services. You can check websites (such as www.travelmar.it, www.alicost.it, and www.gescab.it), but it's smartest to confirm locally—the region's TIs hand out current schedules. Buy tickets on the dock.

AMALFI COAST

I've listed some representative in-season connections for boats from Positano in 2015. Check locally for schedules from Amalfi. If you're thinking of taking a Capri trip from Positano or Amalfi, consider a boat that goes directly to the Blue Grotto (rather than dropping you in the port to catch another boat from there). *Note:* Boats from Sorrento to Positano and Amalfi may not be running; if they aren't, change boats in Capri to reach Amalfi Coast destinations.

From Positano: The last boats often leave Positano before 18:00. There's no real dock, so stormy weather can disrupt schedules. To **Amalfi** (4-8/day, 30 minutes, TravelMar), **Capri** (mid-April-mid-Oct, 2-4/day, 30-60 minutes, Gescab), **Sorrento** (mid-April-mid-Oct only, 2-4/day, 35 minutes, Alicost), **Salerno** (mid-April-Sept only, 4-6/day, 70 minutes, TravelMar).

By Taxi

Given the hairy driving, impossible parking, congested buses, and potential fun, you might consider splurging to hire your own car and driver for the Amalfi day. (Don't bother for Pompeii, as the Circumvesuviana train serves it conveniently and only licensed guides can take you into the site.)

The **Monetti family** car-and-driver service—Raffaele, brother-in-law Tony, and cousin Lorenzo—have taken excellent care of my readers' transit needs for decades. Sample trips and rates: all-day Amalfi Coast (Positano, Amalfi, Ravello), 8 hours, €280; Amalfi Coast and Paestum, 10 hours, €400; transfer to Naples airport or train station to Sorrento, €110 (these prices are for up to four people, more for a larger eight-seater van). Though Sorrento-based, they also do trips from Naples (more expensive). Payment is by cash only (as with most of the car services listed). Their reservation system is simple and reliable (Raffaele's mobile 335-602-9158 or 338-946-2860, "office" run by his English-speaking Finnish wife, Susanna, www.monettitaxi17.it, monettitaxi17@libero.it). Don't just hop into any taxi claiming to be a Monetti—call first. If you get into any kind of a serious jam in the area, you can call Raffaele for help.

Francesco del Pizzo is another smooth and honest driver. A classy young man who speaks English well, Francesco enjoys explaining things as he drives (9 hours or so in a car with up to 4 passengers, €280; up to 8 passengers in a minibus, €320; mobile 333-238-4144, francescodelpizzo@yahoo.it).

Umberto and Giovanni Benvenuto offer transport, narrated tours, and shore excursions throughout the Amalfi Coast, as well as to Rome, Naples, Pompeii, and more. They are based in Praiano (near Positano). While as friendly as the Monettis, they're more upmarket and formal, with steeper rates explained on their website (tel. 081-007-2114, mobile 346-684-0226, US tel. 310-424-5640, www.benvenutolimos.com, info@benvenutolimos.com).

Sorrento Silver Star, with professional drivers and comfortable Mercedes cars and vans, offers custom trips throughout the area at prices between the Monettis' and Benvenutos' (tel. 081-877-1224, mobile 339-388-8143, www.sorrentosilverstar.com, luisa@sorrentosilverstar.com, Luisa).

Anthony Buonocore, based in Amalfi, specializes in cruise shore excursions, as well as transfers anywhere in the region in his eight-person Mercedes van (rates vary, tel. 349-441-0336, www.amalfitransfer.com, buonocoreanthony@yahoo.it).

Rides Only: If you're hiring a cabbie off the street for a ride and not a tour, here are sample fares from Sorrento to Positano: up to four people one-way for about €80 in a car, or up to six people for €90 in a minibus. Figure on paying 50 percent more to Amalfi. While taxis must use a meter within a city, a fixed rate is OK otherwise. Negotiate—ask about a round-trip.

BY TOUR

While hiring your own driver is convenient, it's also expensive. To bring the cost down, split the trip—and the bill—with other travelers using this book. Naples-based **Mondo Guide** offers a nine-hour minibus trip that departs from Sorrento and heads down the Amalfi Coast, with brief stops in Positano, Amalfi, and Ravello, before returning to Sorrento (€50/person). They also offer Rick Steves readers shared tours in Pompeii and in Naples.

Amalfi Coast Bus Tour

The bus trip from Sorrento to Salerno is one of the all-time great white-knuckle rides. Gasp from the right side of the bus as you go

out and from the left as you return to Sorrento. (Those on the wrong side really miss out.) Traffic is so heavy that private tour buses are only allowed to go in one direction (southbound from Sorrento). Summer traffic is infuriating. Fluorescent-vested policemen are posted at

AMALFI COAST

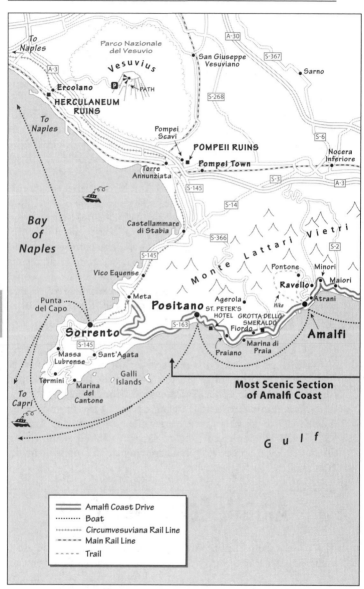

tough bends during peak hours to help fold in side-view mirrors and keep things moving. Here's a loose, self-guided tour of what you're seeing as you travel from west to east.

● **Self-Guided Tour:** Leaving **Sorrento,** the road winds up into the hills past lemon groves and hidden houses. The gray-green trees are olives. (Notice the green nets slung around the trunks; these are unfurled in October and November, when the ripe ol-

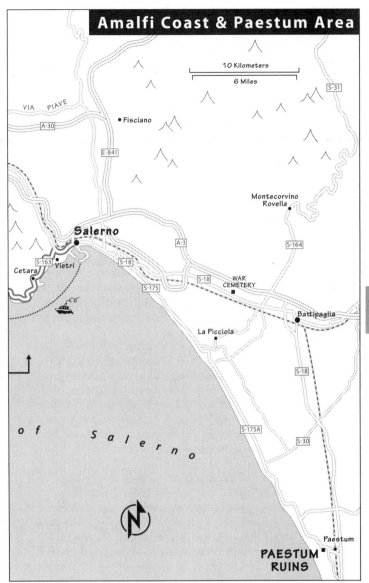

Amalfi Coast & Paestum Area

10 Kilometers

6 Miles

VIA PIAVE

A-30

E-841

Fisciano

Montecorvino Rovella

Salerno

S-31

S-164

A-3

Cetara

S-163

Vietri

S-18

S-18

WAR CEMETERY

S-175

Battipaglia

La Picciola

S-18

o f   S a l e r n o

S-175A

S-30

Paestum

PAESTUM RUINS

ives drop naturally, for an easy self-harvest.) Dark, green-leafed trees planted in dense groves are the source of the region's lemons (many destined to become *limoncello* liqueur) and big, fat citrons (*cedri,* mostly used for marmalade). The black nets over the orange and lemon groves create a greenhouse effect, trapping warmth and humidity for maximum tastiness, while offering protection from extreme weather (preserving the peels used for *limoncello*).

Atop the ridge outside of Sorrento, look to your right: The two small islands after Sorrento are the **Li Galli Islands;** the bigger one, on the left, is Ulysses Island. These islands, once owned by the famed ballet dancer Rudolf Nureyev, mark the boundary between the Bay of Naples and the Bay of Salerno. Technically, the Amalfi Coast drive begins here.

One of the islands also has the first of many stony watchtowers you'll see all along the coast. These were strategically placed within sight of each other, so that a relay of rooftop bonfires could quickly spread word of a Saracen (Turkish pirate) attack.

The limestone cliffs that plunge into the sea were traversed by a hand-carved trail that became a modern road in the mid-19th century. Fruit stands sell produce from farms and orchards just over the hill. Limestone absorbs the heat and rainwater, making this south-facing coastline a fertile suntrap, with temperatures as much as 10 degrees higher than in nearby Sorrento. The chalky, reflective limestone, which extends below the surface, accounts for the uniquely colorful blues and greens of the water. Bougainvillea, geraniums, oleander, and wisteria grow like weeds here in the summer. Notice the nets pulled tight against the cliffs—they're designed to catch rocks that often tumble loose after absorbing heavy rains.

As you approach the exotic-looking town of **Positano,** you know you've reached the scenic heart of the Amalfi Coast. Views of Positano, the main stop along the coast, are dramatic on either side of town. Notice that the town is built on a series of manmade terraces, which were carefully carved out of the steep rock, then filled with fertile soil carried here from Sorrento on the backs of donkeys. You can read the history of the region in Positano's rooftops—a mix of Roman-style red terracotta tiles and white domes inspired by the Saracens.

If you're getting off here, stay on through the first stop by the round-domed yellow church (Chiesa Nova), which is a very long walk above town. Instead, get off at the second stop, Sponda, then head downhill toward the start of my self-guided Positano Walk. Sponda is also the best place to catch the onward bus to Amalfi. If you're coming on a smaller minibus, you'll twist all the way down—seemingly going in circles—to the start of the walk.

Just south of Positano, **St. Peter's Hotel** (Il San Pietro di Positano, camouflaged below the tiny St. Peter's church) is just about the most posh stop on the coast. In the adjacent gorge, notice the hotel's terraced gardens (where they grow produce for their restaurant) above an elevator-accessible beach and dock.

Just around the bend, **Praiano** comes into view. Less ritzy or charming than Positano or Amalfi, it's notable for its huge Cathedral of San Genarro, with a characteristic majolica-tiled roof and dome—a reminder of this region's respected ceramics industry. In spindly Praiano, most of the homes are accessible only by tiny footpaths and staircases. Near the end of town, just before the big tunnel, watch on the left for the big *presepi* (manger scene) embedded into the cliff face. This Praiano-in-miniature was carved by one local man over several decades. At Christmastime, each house is filled with little figures and twinkle lights.

Just past the tunnel, look below and on the right to see another Saracen watchtower. (Yet another caps the little point on the horizon.)

A bit farther along, look down to see the fishing hamlet of **Marina di Praia** tucked into the gorge *(furore)* between two tunnels. If

you're driving—or being driven—consider a detour down here for a coffee break or meal. This serene, tidy nook has its own little pebbly beach with great views of the stout bluffs and watchtower that hem it in. A seafront walkway curls around the bluff all the way to the tower.

Just after going through the next tunnel, watch for a jagged rock formation on its own little pedestal. Locals see the face of the Virgin Mary in this natural feature, and say that she's holding a flower (the tree growing out to the right). Also notice several caged, cantilevered parking pads sticking out from the road. This stretch of coastline is popular for long-term villa rentals—Italians who want to really settle in to Amalfi life.

Look down and left for the blink-or-you'll-miss-it fishing village that's aptly named **Fiordo** ("fjord"), filling yet another gorge. You'll see humble homes burrowed into the cliff face, tucked so far into the gorge that they're entirely in shadows for much of the year. Today these are rented out to vacationers; the postage-stamp beach is uncrowded and inviting.

After the next tunnel, in the following hamlet keep an eye out for donkeys with big baskets on their backs—the only way to make heavy deliveries to homes high in the rocky hills.

Soon you'll pass the big-for-Amalfi parking lot of the **Grotta dello Smeraldo** ("Emerald Grotto"), a cheesy roadside attraction that wrings the most it can out of a pretty, seawater-filled cave. Passing tourists park here and pay to take an elevator down to sea level, pile into big rowboats, and get paddled around a genuinely impressive cavern while the boatman imparts sparse factoids. Unless you've got time to kill, skip it.

Now you're approaching what might be the most dramatic watchtower on the coast, perched atop a near-island. This tower guarded the harbor of the Amalfi navy until the fleet was destroyed in 1343 by a tsunami caused by an earthquake, which also led to Amalfi's decline (it was once one of Italy's leading powers).

Around the next bend you're treated to stunning views of the coastline's namesake—**Amalfi.** The white villa sitting on the low point between here and there (with another watchtower at its tip) once belonged to Sophia Loren. Now pan up to the very top of the steep, steep cliffs overhead. The hulking former Monastery of Santa Rosa occupies this prime territory. Locals proudly explain that the *sfogliatella* dessert so beloved throughout the Campania region was first created at this monastery. (Today it's a luxury re-sort, where you can pay a premium to sleep in a tight little former monk's cell.)

The most striking stretch of coastline ends where the bus pulls to a halt—at the end of the line, the waterfront of Amalfi town. Spend some time enjoying this once-powerful, now-pleasant city, with its fine cathedral, fascinating paper museum, and fun-to-explore tangle of lanes (covered later in this chapter).

From Amalfi, you can transfer to another bus to either head up to **Ravello** (described later), capping a cliff just beyond Amalfi, or onward to the big city of **Salerno**. Alternatively, buses and boats take you back to Positano and Sorrento.

If you're continuing the trip southward (on the bus to Salerno or Ravello), look up to the left as you leave Amalfi—the white house that clings to a cliff (Villa Rondinaia) was home for many years to writer Gore Vidal. Soon you'll pass through the low-impact, pleasantly untouristy town of **Atrani**. From here, you'll enjoy fine (though slightly less thrilling) scenery along the western half of the Amalfi Coast all the way to Salerno.

Positano

According to legend, the Greek god Poseidon created Positano for Pasitea, a nymph he lusted after. History says the town was founded when ancient Greeks at Paestum decided to move out of the swamp (to escape the malaria carried by its mosquitoes). Specializing in scenery and sand, Positano hangs halfway between Sorrento and Amalfi town on the most spectacular stretch of the coast.

In antiquity, Positano was famed for its bold sailors and hearty fleet. But after a big 1343 tsunami and the pirate raids of the Middle Ages, its wealth and power declined. It flourished again as a favorite under the Bourbon royal family in the 1700s, when many of its fine mansions were built. Until the late 1800s, the only access was by donkey path or by sea. In the 20th century, Positano became a haven for artists and writers escaping Communist Russia or Nazi Germany. In 1953, American writer John Steinbeck's essay on the town popularized Positano among tourists, and soon after it became a trendy Riviera stop. That was when the town gave the world "Moda Positano"—a leisurely *dolce vita* lifestyle of walking barefoot; wearing bright, happy, colorful clothes; and sporting skimpy bikinis.

Today, the village, a breathtaking sight from a distance, is a pleasant gathering of cafés and expensive stores draped over an almost comically steep hillside. Terraced gardens and historic houses cascade downhill to a stately cathedral and a broad, pebbly beach. Positano is famous for its fashions—and 90 percent of its shops are women's clothing boutiques (linen is a particularly popular item).

The "skyline" looks like it did a century ago. Notice the town's characteristic Saracen-inspired rooftop domes. Filled with sand, these provide low-tech insulation—to help buildings in the days before air-conditioning stay cool in summer and warm in winter. Traditionally, they were painted white in summer and black in winter.

It's been practically impossible to get a building permit in Positano for over 25 years now, and landowners who want to renovate can't make external changes. Endless staircases are a way of life for the 4,000 hardy locals. Only one street in Positano allows motorized traffic; the rest are narrow pedestrian lanes. Because hotels don't take large groups (bus access is too difficult), this town—unlike Sorrento—has been spared the ravages of big-bus tourism.

Consider seeing Positano as a day trip from Sorrento: Take the bus out and the afternoon ferry home, but be sure to check the boat schedules when you arrive—the last ferry often leaves before 18:00, and doesn't always run in spring and fall. Or spend the night to enjoy the magic of Positano. The town has a local flavor at night, when the grown-ups stroll and the kids play soccer on the church porch.

Orientation to Positano

Squished into a ravine, with narrow alleys that cascade down to the harbor, Positano requires you to stroll, whether you're going up or heading down. The center of town has no main square (unless you count the beach). There's little to do here but eat, window-shop, and enjoy the beach and views...hence the town's popularity.

TOURIST INFORMATION

The TI is a block from the beach, in the red building a half-block beyond the bottom of the church steps (April-Sept Mon-Sat 9:00-18:00 or later, Sun 9:00-14:00, shorter hours off-season, Via Regina Giovanna 13, tel. 089-875-067, www.aziendaturismopositano.it).

Local Guide: Lucia Ferrara (a.k.a. "Zia Lucy") is a Positano native who brings substance to this glitzy town. During the day, she leads guided hiking tours, including the "Path of the Gods" above Amalfi town (about 4 miles, 4 hours, €45-55/person); in the afternoons and evenings, she leads town walking tours (3 hours, €30/person; ask about possible food tours of Positano, contact for specific rates and schedules, mobile 339-272-0971, info@zialucy.it, www.zialucy.it).

ARRIVAL IN POSITANO

The main coast highway winds above the town. Regional SITA buses (often red or green-and-white) stop at two scheduled bus stops located at either end of town: Chiesa Nuova (at Bar Internazionale, near the Sorrento end of town; use this one only if you're staying at Brikette Hostel) and Sponda (nearer Amalfi town). Although both stops are near roads leading downhill through the town to the beach, Sponda is closer and less steep; from this stop, it's a scenic 20-minute downhill stroll/shop/munch to the beach (and TI).

Neither bus stop has **baggage storage,** which makes it hard to visit Positano on the way (for example, between overnights in Sorrento and Amalfi). A luggage service called Blu Porter can meet you at the Sponda bus stop and watch your bags for you for €5 apiece—but you have to call them in advance (tel. 089-811-496). If you can't reach them, your best bet is to get off at Chiesa Nuova and head for the Brikette Hostel, which offers day privileges for €10, including luggage storage, Wi-Fi, and showers. A last resort is to get off at the Sponda stop and roll your bags all the way down to Piazza dei Mulini, where the porters tend to hang out.

If you're catching the SITA bus back to Sorrento, be aware that it may leave from the Sponda stop up to five minutes before the printed departure. There's simply no room for the bus to wait, so in case the driver is early, you should be, too (about hourly, daily 7:00-22:00, until 20:00 off-season). Buy tickets at the tobacco shop in the town center (on Piazza dei Mulini) or just below the Sponda bus stop at the Li Galli Bar or Total gas station (across from Hotel Marincanto).

If the walk up to the stop is too tough, take the dizzy little local red-and-white shuttle bus (marked *Interno Positano*), which constantly loops through Positano, connecting the lower town with the highway's two bus stops (2/hour, €1.30 at tobacco shop on Piazza dei Mulini, €1.70 on board, catch it at convenient stop at the corner of Via Colombo and Via dei Mulini, heads up to Sponda). Collina Bakery, located off Piazza dei Mulini (as close as cars, taxis, and the shuttle bus can get to the beach), is just across from the shuttle bus stop, with a fine, breezy terrace to enjoy while you wait.

Drivers must go with the one-way flow, entering the town only at the Chiesa Nuova bus stop (closest to Sorrento) and exiting at Sponda. Driving is a headache here. Parking is even worse.

Positano Walk

While there's no real sightseeing in Positano, this short, self-guided stroll downhill will help you get your bearings from top to bottom.
• *Start at...*

Piazza dei Mulini: This is the upper-town meeting point—as close to the beach as vehicles can get—and the lower stop for the little red-and-white shuttle bus. Collina Bakery is a local hangout (in this small town, gossiping is a big pastime)—older people tend to gather inside, while the younger crowd congregates on the wisteria-draped terrace across the street. The terrace also shades the best *granita* (lemon slush) stand in town, where the family has been following the same secret recipe for generations.

Dip into the little yellow Church of the Holy Rosary (by the road), with a serene 12th-century interior. Up front, to the right of the main altar, find the delicately carved fragment of a Roman sarcophagus (first century B.C.). Positano sits upon the site of a sprawling Roman villa, and we'll see a scant few reminders of that age as we walk.

Now continue downhill into town, passing a variety of shops—many selling linen and ceramics. These industries boomed when tourists discovered Positano in the 1970s. The beach-inspired Moda Positano fashion label was born as a break from the rigid dress code of the '50s. For tips on shopping for linen (and other things), see "Shopping in Positano," later. Positano also considers itself an artists' colony, so you'll see many galleries featuring the work of area artists.
• *Wander downhill to the "fork" in the road (stairs to the left, road to the right). You've reached...*

Midtown: At Enoteca Cuomo (#3), butchers Pasquale and Rosario stock fine local red wines and are happy to explain their virtues. They also make homemade sausages, salami, and *panini*—

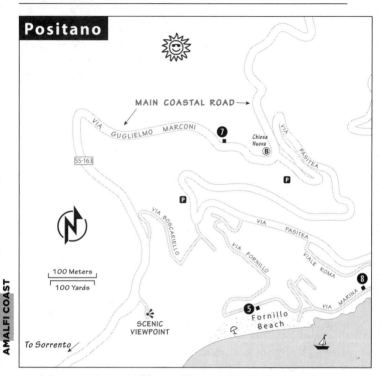

good for a quick lunch. The smaller set of stairs leads to the rec-ommended Delicatessen grocery store, where Emilia can fix you a good picnic (see "Eating in Positano," later).

La Zagara (across the lane from the steps, at #10) is a pricey pastry shop by day and a piano bar by night. Tempting pastries such as the rum-drenched *babà* (a southern Italian favorite) fill the window display. After hours, it's filled with traditional Nea-politan music and dancing. A bit farther downhill, Brunella (on the right, at #24) is respected for traditional, quality, and locally made linens.

Across the street, Hotel Palazzo Murat fills what was once a grand Benedictine monastery. Napoleon, fearing the power of the Church, had many such monasteries closed during his rule here. This one became a private palace, named for his brother-in-law, who was briefly the King of Naples. Step into the plush courtyard to enjoy the scene, with great views of the cathedral's majolica-slathered dome. Continuing on, under a fragrant wisteria trellis, you'll pass "street merchants' gulch," where artisans display their goodies.

• Continue straight down. You'll run into a fork at the big church. For now, turn right and go downstairs to Piazza Flavio Gioia, facing the big...

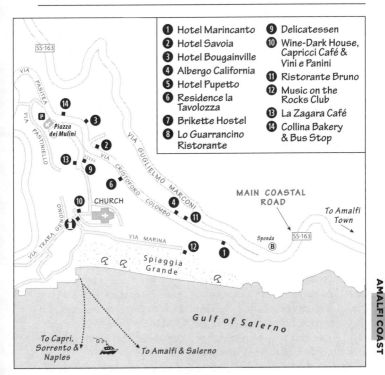

1 Hotel Marincanto
2 Hotel Savoia
3 Hotel Bougainville
4 Albergo California
5 Hotel Pupetto
6 Residence la Tavolozza
7 Brikette Hostel
8 Lo Guarrancino Ristorante
9 Delicatessen
10 Wine-Dark House, Capricci Café & Vini e Panini
11 Ristorante Bruno
12 Music on the Rocks Club
13 La Zagara Café
14 Collina Bakery & Bus Stop

AMALFI COAST

Church of Santa Maria Assunta: This church, which sits upon Roman ruins, was once the abbey of Positano's 12th-century Benedictine monastery. Originally Romanesque, it was eventually abandoned (along with the entire lower town) out of fear of pirate attacks. When the coast was clear in the 18th century, the church was given an extreme Baroque makeover.

Step **inside**. Renovation may be under way when you visit; try to find these items: In the first chapel on the left is a fine manger scene *(presepe)*. Its original 18th-century figurines give you an idea of the folk costumes of the age. Above the main altar is the Black Madonna, an icon-like Byzantine painting, which was likely brought here in the 12th century by Benedictine monks. But locals prefer the romantic legend: Saracen pirates had it on their ship as plunder. A violent storm hit—sure to sink the evil ship. The painting of Mary spoke, saying, *"Posa, posa"* (lay me down), and the ship glided safely to this harbor. The pirates were so stricken they became Christians. Locals kept the painting, and the town became known as *Posa-tano* (recalling Mary's command). To the right of the altar, a small freestanding display case holds a silver and copper bust of St. Vitus—the town patron, who brought Christianity here in about A.D. 300. In the adjacent niche (on the right) is a rare 1599 painting by Fabrizio Santafede of Baby Jesus being circumcised, considered the finest historic painting in town.

Back outside, you'll see the **bell tower,** dating from 1707. Above the door, it sports a Romanesque relief scavenged from the original church. The scene—a wolf mermaid with seven little fish—was a reminder to worshippers of how integral the sea was to their livelihood. Notice the characteristic shallow, white "insulation domes" on rooftops in front of the church.

• *Backtrack up the steps, circling around the church. You'll likely see a construction zone, and possibly a new museum.*

The entire town center of today's Positano—from this cathedral all the way up to the Piazza dei Mulini, where we started this walk—sits upon the site of a huge **Roman villa complex,** buried when Mount Vesuvius erupted in A.D. 79. (While landlocked Pompeii and Herculaneum were working-class merchant cities, prime seafront property like this was used for luxuriating.) Positano recently began excavating one small part of the villa, and a small museum planned here will provide views of a surviving fragment of a large Roman fresco. You may also be able to take the stairs down to two glass doors that offer a peek into the church's crypt—originally the early church's altar. According to local legend, the Benedictines sat their dead brothers on the stone choir chairs here to decompose and remind all of their mortality.

• *Continue climbing down the steps arcing to the right (following* beach/ spiaggia *signs). You'll eventually come to the little square, with concrete benches, facing the beach.*

Piazzetta: This is the town gathering point in the evening, as local boys hustle tourist girls into the nearby nightclub. Residents traded their historic baptistery font with Amalfi town for the two iron lions you see facing the beach. Around the staircase, you'll also see some original Roman columns, scavenged from the buried villa. Look up and admire the colorful majolica tiles so typical of church domes in this region.

Positano was once a notable naval power, with many shipyards along this beach. These eventually became fishermen's quarters and storehouses, and later, today's tourist restaurants. The Positano **beach,** called Spiaggia Grande, is half public (straight ahead) and half private (to the left, behind the little fence). It's atmospherically littered with resting fishing boats. The big kiosk on the beach straight ahead sells excursions to Capri and elsewhere.

Looking out over the beach, from this point you can see three of the **watchtowers** built centuries ago to protect the Amalfi Coast from Saracen pirates: one on the far-left horizon, just below Praiano; a small one on the Galli Islands, straight ahead; and the rectangular one far to the right, marking the end of Fornillo Beach. (The round tower in the foreground is modern.)

Defenders used these towers—strategically situated within sight of each other—to relay smoke signals. In more recent times, the tower on the right (near Fornillo Beach) was a hangout for artists, who holed up inside for inspiration. (The people of Positano pride themselves on being artists rather than snazzy jet-setters like those in Capri.)

As you face out to sea, on the far-left side of the beach (below Rada Restaurant) is **Music on the Rocks,** a chic club that's the only remaining piece of the 1970s scene, when Positano really rocked. While it's dead until about 23:00, if you just want to stop for a drink, the cool troglo-disco interior opens at 21:00.

• *Now turn right and wander across the beach. Behind the kiosks that sell boat tickets, find the steps up to the path that climbs up and over, past a 13th-century lookout fort from Saracen pirate days, to the next beach. It's a worthwhile little five-minute walk to...*

Fornillo Beach: This is where locals go for better swimming and to escape some of the tourist crowds. The walk over offers a welcome change of scene, as the path winds through a shady ravine.

• *Our walk is over. Time to relax.*

Sights in Positano

Beaches

Positano's pebbly and sandy primary beach, **Spiaggia Grande,** is colorful with umbrellas as it stretches wide around the cove. It's mostly private (pay to enter, includes lounge chair and umbrella), with a free section near the middle, close to where the boats take off. Look for the pay showers. The nearest WC is beneath the steps to the right (as you face the water).

Fornillo Beach, a less-crowded option just around the bend (to the west) of Spiaggia Grande, is favored by residents, with more affordable chair/umbrella rentals. It has a mellow Robinson Crusoe vibe, with a sturdy Saracen tower keeping watch overhead. This beach has a few humble snack bars and lunch eateries. Note that its position, tucked back in the rocks, means it gets shade earlier in the day than the main beach.

Boat Trips

At the west end of Spiaggia Grande (to the right as you face the sea), booths sell tickets to a number of destinations. Consider renting a rowboat, or see if they can talk you into taking a boat tour.

Ferries run to Amalfi, Capri, and Sorrento.

Shopping

Linen: Garments made of **linen** (especially women's dresses) are popular items in Positano. To find a good-quality piece that will last, look for "Made in Positano" (or at least "Made in Italy") on

AMALFI COAST

Sleep Code

Abbreviations   (€1=about $1.10, country code: 39)
S=Single, **D**=Double/Twin, **T**=Triple, **Q**=Quad, **b**=bathroom

Price Rankings

  $$$ Higher Priced—Most rooms €180 or more
   $$ Moderately Priced—Most rooms €130-180
    $ Lower Priced—Most rooms €130 or less

Unless otherwise noted, credit cards are accepted, breakfast is included, free Wi-Fi and/or a guest computer is generally available, and English is spoken. Many towns in Italy levy a hotel tax of €1.50-5 per person, per night (often collected in cash; usually not included in the rates I've quoted). Prices change; verify current rates online or by email. For the best prices, book directly with the hotel.

the label, and check the percentage of linen; 60 percent or more is excellent quality. Two companies with top reputations and multiple outlets are **Brunella** and **Pepito's** (each has shops on Via Colombo, near the top of town; along Via Pasitea, the main drag; and along claustrophobic Saraceno lane, near the bottom of town, parallel to the beach).

Ceramics: Ceramica Assunta, one of the oldest ceramics stores in Positano, carries colorful Solimene dinnerware and more at two locations (Via Colombo 97 and Via Colombo 137).

Custom Sandals: Positano has a tradition of handmade sandals, crafted to your specifications while you wait (prices start at about €50). One good shop, La Botteguccia, faces the tranquil little square just up from the TI; around the corner, in front of the Capricci restaurant, you'll see Carmine Todisco, who loves to explain how his grandfather shod Jackie O.

Nightlife

The big-time action in the old town center is the impressive club **Music on the Rocks,** literally carved into the rocks on the beach (opens at 21:00 mid-April-Oct but party starts about 23:30, €10-20 cover charge in summer includes a drink, go to dance or just check out the scene, Via Grotte Dell'Incanto 51, tel. 089-875-874, www.musicontherocks.it). For a more low-key atmosphere, café/pastry shop **La Zagara** hosts music nightly in summer (starts around 21:00, Via dei Mulini 10, tel. 089-875-964).

Sleeping in Positano

These hotels (with the exceptions of the hostel and Hotel Pupetto) are all on or near Via Colombo, which leads from the Sponda bus stop down into the village. Prices given are for the highest season (May-Sept)—at other times, they become soft. Most places close in the winter (Dec-Feb or longer). Expect to pay more than €20 a day to park, except at Albergo California.

$$$ Hotel Marincanto is a recently restored, somewhat impersonal four-star hotel with 32 beautiful rooms and a bright breakfast terrace practically teetering on a cliff. Suites seem to be designed for a *luna di miele*—honeymoon (Db-€230, more expensive superior rooms and suites, extra bed-€70, air-con, elevator, pool, stairs down to a private beach, parking-€28/day, closed Nov-March, 50 yards below Sponda bus stop at Via Colombo 50, reception on bottom floor, tel. 089-875-130, www.marincanto.it, info@marincanto.it).

$$ Hotel Savoia, run by the friendly D'Aiello family, has 39 sizeable, breezy, bright, simple, tiled rooms (viewless Db-€140, view Db-€180, deluxe Db with balcony or terrace-€210, for the best rate book direct and show the current edition of this book, extra bed-€50, air-con, elevator, closed Nov-Feb, Via Colombo 73, tel. 089-875-003, www.savoiapositano.it, info@savoiapositano.it).

$$ Hotel Bougainville rents 16 comfortable rooms, half with balconies. Everything's bright, modern, and tasteful (small-windowed viewless economy Db-€120, regular viewless Db-€160, view Db-€195, 5 percent off these rates in 2016 if you book direct and show this book, check website for specials, air-con, small elevator, closed Nov-March, Via Colombo 25, tel. 089-875-047, www.bougainville.it, info@bougainville.it, friendly Marella).

$$ Albergo California has 15 spacious rooms (all with lofty views), a grand terrace draped with vines, and full breakfasts. The Cinque family—including Maria, Bronx-born son John, and grandchildren Giuseppe and Maria—will welcome you (view Db-€170 June-Sept, €10 less April-May and Oct, these prices promised with this book through 2016, air-con, free parking, closed Nov-Easter, Via Colombo 141, tel. 089-875-382, www.hotelcaliforniapositano.it, info@hotelcaliforniapositano.it).

$$ Hotel Pupetto, facing the secluded Fornillo Beach (a 10-minute walk from Positano's bustling harbor), is a family-run hotel for beach lovers. Its 38 rooms are spartan and pricey, but all come with balconies (viewless Db-€160, view Db-€180, superior Db with seaview terrace-€240, air-con, elevator, drivers park high above and hike down—call for porter service, Via Fornillo 37, tel. 089-875-087, www.hotelpupetto.it, info@hotelpupetto.it).

$ Residence la Tavolozza is an attractive six-room hotel,

AMALFI COAST

warmly run by Celeste (cheh-LEHS-tay) and daughters Francesca (who speaks English) and Paola. Each cheerily tiled room comes with a view, a terrace, and silence (Db-€95-120 depending on size, extra for lavish à la carte breakfast, these prices promised through 2016 with this book, families can ask for sprawling "Royal Apartment"—price varies with number of people, call to confirm if arriving late, air-con, closed Dec-Feb, Via Colombo 10, tel. 089-875-040, www.latavolozzapositano.it, info@latavolozzapositano.it).

$ **Brikette Hostel** offers your best cheap dorm-bed option in this otherwise ritzy town. Renting 35 pricey-for-a-dorm beds and offering a great sun and breakfast terrace, it has a loose, youthful, rough-around-the-edges ambience (bunk in dorm room-€38-54, Db-€165, bigger family rooms; breakfast-€5, €5-7 dinners; air-con in a few rooms; day privileges for day-trippers, including luggage storage-€10; leave bus at Chiesa Nuova/Bar Internazionale stop and backtrack uphill 500 feet to Via G. Marconi 358, www.hostel-positano.com, hostelpositano@gmail.com). The hostel isn't available by phone; email instead.

Eating in Positano

On the Beach: At the waterfront, several interchangeable restaurants with view terraces leave people fat and happy, albeit with

skinnier wallets (figure €15-20 pastas and *secondi,* plus pricey drinks and sides, and a cover charge). Little distinguishes one place from the next; all are scenic, convenient, and overpriced.

Near the Beach: Lo Guarrancino, hidden on the path to Fornillo Beach, is a local favorite for its great views and good food at prices similar to the beachfront places (€12-13 pizzas, €12-23 pastas and *secondi,* daily 12:00-15:30 & 19:00-23:00, closed Nov-Easter, follow path behind the boat-ticket kiosks 5 minutes to Via Positanesi d'America 12, tel. 089-875-794). **Wine-Dark House,** tucked around the corner from the beach (and the TI), fills a cute little piazzetta at the start of Saraceno lane. They serve good food (€10-20 pastas and *secondi*), have a respect for wine (several local wines-€5/glass), and are popular with Positano's youngsters for their long list of €6-7 sandwiches (closed Tue, Via del Saraceno 6/8, tel. 089-811-925). Next door, **Capricci** is budget-priced (for downtown Positano). This informal café and *tavola calda* serves up €7-9 pizza and main courses that you can eat on the spot (at a long counter overlooking the beach) or take away. If you sit down at their white-tablecloth restaurant across the street, you get the same food but the prices go up (daily 9:00-23:00, Via Regina Giovanna 12, delivery available, tel. 089-812-145, www.capriccipositano.it).

Picnics: If a picnic dinner on your balcony or the beach sounds good, sunny Emilia at the **Delicatessen** grocery store can supply the ingredients: *antipasto misto,* pastas, home-cooked dishes, and sandwiches made to order. She'll heat it up for you and throw in the picnic ware. Come early for the best selection (all sold by weight, daily 7:00-22:00, shorter hours off-season, just below car park at Via del Mulini 5, tel. 089-875-489). **Vini e Panini,** another small grocery, is a block from the beach a few steps above the TI. Daniela, the fifth-generation owner, speaks English and happily makes sandwiches to order. Choose from the "Caprese" (mozzarella and tomato), the "Positano" (mozzarella, tomato, and prosciutto), or create your own (€4-6 each). They also have a nice selection of well-priced regional wines (daily 8:00-20:00, until 22:00 in summer, closed mid-Nov-mid-March, just off church steps, tel. 089-875-175).

"Uptown": The unassuming, family-run **Ristorante Bruno** is handy to my listed hotels. While pricey for what it is, it's worth considering if you want a meal without hiking down into the town center (€12-17 pastas, €17-22 *secondi,* daily 12:30-23:00, closed Nov-Easter, near the top of Via Colombo at #157, tel. 089-875-179).

AMALFI COAST

Amalfi Town

After Rome fell, the Amalfi Coast's namesake town was one of the first to trade goods—coffee, carpets, and paper—between Europe and points east. Its heyday

was the 10th and 11th centuries, when it was a powerful maritime republic—a trading power with a fleet that controlled this region and rivaled Pisa, Genoa, and Venice. The Republic of Amalfi founded a hospital in Jerusalem and claims to have founded the Knights of Malta order—even giving them the Amalfi cross, which became the famous Maltese cross. Amalfi minted its own coins and established "rules of the sea"—the basics of which survive today.

In 1343, this little powerhouse was suddenly destroyed by a tsunami caused by an undersea earthquake. That disaster, compounded by devastating plagues, left Amalfi a humble backwater.

Much of the culture of this entire region was driven by this town—but because it fell from power, Amalfi doesn't always get the credit it deserves. Today its 5,000 residents live off tourism. Amalfi is not as picturesque as Positano or as well-connected as Sorrento, but it has a real-city feel and a vivacious bustle. Take some time to explore the town.

Amalfi's one main street runs up from the waterfront through a deep valley, with stairways to courtyards and houses on either side. It's worth walking uphill to the workaday upper end of town. Super-atmospheric, narrow, stepped side lanes branch off, squeezing between hulking old buildings. If you hear water under a grate in the main street, it's the creek that runs through the ravine—a reminder that, originally, the town straddled the stream, and later paved over it to create a main drag. As you return downhill, be sure to explore up the winding and narrow lanes and arcaded passages on either side of the main street.

Though less touristy than Positano, Amalfi is packed during the day with big-bus tours (whose drivers pay €50 an hour to park while their groups shop for *limoncello* and ceramics). Amalfi's charms reveal themselves early and late in the day, when the tourist crowds dissipate.

Orientation to Amalfi Town

Amalfi's waterfront is the coast's biggest transport hub. The bus station, ferry docks, and a parking lot (€5/hour; if the lot is full, park in the huge Lunarossa garage, burrowed into the hillside just past town, before Atrani) are next to each other. They are overlooked by a statue of local boy Flavio Gioia, the purported inventor of the magnetic compass. Amalfi's TI is just up the main road, right before the post office and overlooking the beach.

Before you enter the town, notice the colorful tile above the Porta della Marina gateway, showing off the trading domain of the maritime Republic of Amalfi. Just to the left, along the busy road, is a series of arches that indicate the long, narrow, vaulted halls of its arsenal—where ships were built in the 11th century. One of these is now the fine little Arsenal Museum (described later).

Venture into the town and you'll quickly come to **Piazza Duomo,** the main square, sporting a spring water-spewing statue of St. Andrew, and the cathedral—the town's most important sight.

The farther you get away from the water, the more traditional Amalfi becomes. The Paper Museum is a 10-minute walk up Via Lorenzo d'Amalfi, the main drag. From here, the road narrows and you can turn off onto a path leading to the shaded Valle dei Mulini; it's full of paper-mill ruins that recall this once proud and prosper-

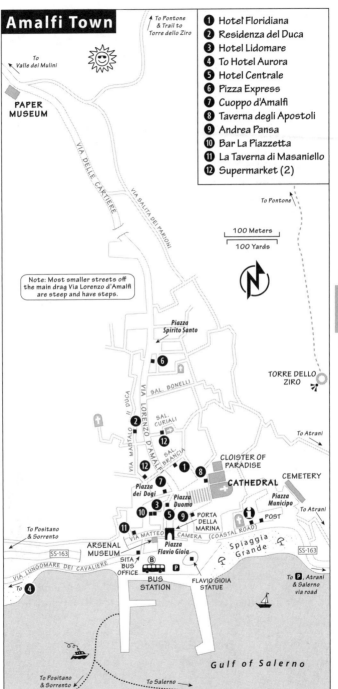

Amalfi Town

To Pontone
& Trail to
Torre dello Ziro

To
Valle dei Mulini

1 Hotel Floridiana
2 Residenza del Duca
3 Hotel Lidomare
4 To Hotel Aurora
5 Hotel Centrale
6 Pizza Express
7 Cuoppo d'Amalfi
8 Taverna degli Apostoli
9 Andrea Pansa
10 Bar La Piazzetta
11 La Taverna di Masaniello
12 Supermarket (2)

PAPER MUSEUM

VIA DELLE CARTIERE

VIA SALITA DEI PARIONI

To Pontone

100 Meters
100 Yards

Note: Most smaller streets off
the main drag Via Lorenzo d'Amalfi
are steep and have steps.

N

AMALFI COAST

Piazza
Spirito Santo

6

VIA LORENZO D'AMALFI

SAL. BONELLI

TORRE DELLO ZIRO

2

SAL. CURIALI

VIA MASTALO II DUCA

12

SAL. BRANCIA

To Atrani

12

1

8

CLOISTER OF PARADISE

CEMETERY

7

CATHEDRAL

Piazza
dei Dogi

Piazza
Duomo

Piazza
Municipo

To Atrani

10

3

5

9

PORTA
DELLA
MARINA

POST

11

VIA MATTEO CAMERA (COASTAL ROAD)

To Positano
& Sorrento

ARSENAL
MUSEUM

SS-163

Piazza
Flavio Gioia

Spiaggia
Grande

SS-163

SITA
BUS
OFFICE

B

P

VIA LUNGOMARE DEI CAVALIERE

To
4

BUS
STATION

FLAVIO GIOIA
STATUE

To P, Atrani
& Salerno
via road

Gulf of Salerno

To Positano
& Sorrento

To Salerno

ous industry. The ruined castle clinging to the rocky ridge above Amalfi is Torre dello Ziro, a good lookout point for intrepid hikers.

TOURIST INFORMATION

The TI is about 100 yards from the bus station and ferry dock, next to the post office; facing the sea, it's to the left (Mon-Fri 9:00-13:00 & 14:30-17:30, Sat 9:00-13:00, closed Sun, shorter hours off-season, pay WC in same courtyard, Corso della Repubbliche Marinare 27, tel. 089-871-107, www.amalfitouristoffice.it).

HELPFUL HINTS

Don't Get Stranded: Be warned—the **last bus** back to Sorrento leaves as early as 20:00 (in Oct-March, but likely somewhat later in other months: June-July at 22:00, Aug at 23:00, April-May and Sept at 21:00—confirm times locally). Especially in summer, that last bus out may be full, leaving your only option a €100 taxi ride.

Baggage Storage: You can store your bag safely for €5 at the **Divina Costiera Travel Office** facing the waterfront square, across from the bus parking area (daily 8:00-13:00 & 14:00-19:00, closed mid-Nov-March, tel. 089-872-467).

Speedboat Charters: To hire your own boat for a tour of the coastline from Amalfi (or to Capri), consider **Charter La Dolce Vita** (mobile 335-549-9365, www.amalficoastyacht.it).

Sights in Amalfi Town

Cathedral

This church is "Amalfi Romanesque" (a mix of Moorish and Byzantine flavors, built c. 1000-1300), with a fanciful Neo-Byzantine facade from the 19th century. Climb the imposing stairway, which functions as a mini Spanish Steps hangout zone and a handy outdoor theater. The 1,000-year-old bronze door at the top was given to Amalfi by a wealthy local merchant who had it made in Constantinople.

Cost and Hours: €3, daily 10:00-17:00, open only for prayer 7:30-10:00 & 17:00-19:30, tel. 089-871-324. There's a fine, free WC at the top of the steps (through unmarked green door, just a few steps before ticket booth, ask for key at desk).

Visiting the Cathedral: Pick up the English brochure as you enter. Visitors are directed on a one-way circuit through the cathedral complex with four stops.

This courtyard of 120 graceful columns—the **"Cloister of**

Paradise"—was the cemetery for nobles in the 13th century (note their stone sarcophagi). Don't miss the fine view of the bell tower and its majolica tiles.

The original ninth-century church, known as the **Basilica of the Crucifix,** boasts a fine 13th-century wooden crucifix. Today the basilica is a museum filled with the cathedral's art treasures. The Angevin Mitre (Mitra Angioina), with a "pavement of tiny pearls" setting off its gold and gems, has been worn by bishops since the 14th century. Also on display (waist-high, facing the altar) is a carved wooden decoration from a Saracen pirate ship that wrecked just outside of town in 1544 during a freak storm. Believers credit St. Andrew with causing the storm that saved the town from certain Turkish pillage and plunder.

Down the stairs to the right of the basilica's altar is the **Crypt of St. Andrew.** Just as Venice needed St. Mark to get on the pilgrimage map, Amalfi needed St. Andrew—one of the apostles who, along with his brother Peter, left their fishing nets to become the original "fishers of men." Under the huge bronze statue, you'll see a reliquary holding what are believed to be Andrew's remains. These were brought here from Constantinople in 1206 during the Crusades—an indication of the wealth and importance of Amalfi back then.

Climb the stairs up into the **cathedral** itself. Behind the main altar is a painting of St. Andrew martyred on an X-shaped cross flanked by two Egyptian granite columns supporting a triumphal arch. Before leaving, check out the delicate mother-of-pearl crucifix (right of door in back).

▲Paper Museum

This excellent little museum—worth ▲▲▲ for engineers—makes for a good excuse to break free from the crowds and walk up the main drag to a quieter, more local part of town. Paper has been a vital industry here since Amalfi's glory days in the Middle Ages. They'd pound rags into pulp in a big vat, pull it up using a screen, and air-dry it to create paper (the same technique used to make the paper sold today in Amalfi shops). At this cavernous, cool 13th-century paper mill-turned-museum, a multilingual guide collects groups at the entrance (no particular times) for a 25-minute tour. The guide recounts the history and process of papermaking and turns on the museum's vintage machinery. You'll see how the Amalfi River (which you can still hear rumbling underfoot) powered this important industry, and learn the origins of the term "watermark." Kids can dip a screen into the rag pool and make a sheet of paper. It's amazing to think this factory produced paper through 1969 (when it was replaced by a modern facility up the valley).

Cost and Hours: €4; March-Oct daily 10:00-18:30; Nov-Feb usually Tue-Sun 10:00-15:30, closed Mon; a 10-minute walk up the main street from the cathedral, look for signs to *Museo della Carta;* tel. 089-830-4561, www.museodellacarta.it. On the way up to the museum, don't miss the huge, outdoor *presepi* (Nativity scenes) on your left.

Arsenal Museum

This small, underground museum just across the road from the bus station tells the history of Amalfi's maritime glory years. Stepping into the single long room under the dramatic vaulted stone ceiling, you can just tell that 1,000 years ago, they made ships here. The collection (well-described in English) is small, but there are plenty of historic artifacts from Amalfi's city-state days of independence (839-1135). You'll learn about the early compass "invented" here in 1302, which ultimately opened up exploration of the New World. In 1080, it was written, "This city appears opulent and popular; no other city is as rich in silver, garments, and gold. Here dwells navigators very expert at pointing out the ways of the sea and the sphere of the heavens."

Cost and Hours: €2, Tue-Sun 10:00-13:00 & 16:00-19:00, closed Mon, shorter hours off-season, Piazza Flavio Gioia, mobile 334-917-7814.

Performances: Half of the arsenal space is a venue for performances of *Amalfi Musical,* a 1.5-hour musical bonanza loosely based on local history (English subtitles, 2/week in summer, www.amalfimusical.it).

HIKES

Amalfi is the starting point for several fine hikes, two of which I've described here. The TI hands out photocopies of Giovanni Visetti's trail maps (or you can download them yourself at www.giovis.com). If you can find it, the best book on hiking is Julian Tippett's *Sorrento Amalfi Capri Car Tours and Walks*, with useful color-coded maps and info on public transportation to the trailheads. Lucia Ferrara, a great guide based in Positano, leads hikes around Amalfi.

Hike #1: Pontone

This loop trail leads up the valley past paper-mill ruins, ending in the tiny town of Pontone; you can get lunch there, and head back down to the town of Amalfi (allow 3 hours total). Bring a good map, since it's easy to veer off the main route. Start your hike by following the main road (Via Lorenzo d'Amalfi) away from the sea.

After the Paper Museum, jog right, then left to join the trail, which runs through the shaded woods along a babbling stream. Heed the signs that warn people to stay away from the ruins of paper mills (no matter how tempting they look), since many are ready to collapse on unwary hikers. Continue up to Pontone, where

Trattoria l'Antico Borgo offers wonderful cuisine and a great view (Via Noce 4, tel. 089-871-469). After lunch, return to Amalfi via a steep stairway.

If you're feeling ambitious, before you head back to Amalfi, add a one-hour detour (30 minutes each way) to visit the ridge-hugging **Torre dello Ziro** (ask a local how to find the trail to this tower). You'll be rewarded with a spectacular view.

Hike #2: Atrani

For an easier stroll, head to the nearby town of Atrani. This village, just a 15-minute stroll beyond Amalfi town, is a world apart; its 1,500 residents consider themselves definitely *not* from Amalfi. Leave Amalfi via the main road and stay on the water side until the promenade ends. Cross the street, continue a few more yards, then go up the whitewashed staircase just past the pizzeria. From here, twist up through old lanes to a paved route that takes you over the hill and drops you into Atrani in about 15 minutes.

With relatively few tourists, a delightful town square, and a free, sandy beach (if you drive here, pay for parking at harbor), Atrani has none of Amalfi's trendy resort feel. Piazza Umberto is the core of town, with cafés, restaurants, and little grocery stores that can make sandwiches. A whitewashed staircase leads up to the serene and beautiful town church (under the clock face).

To save time and sweat on the return walk, follow the promenade just above water level toward Amalfi. Then walk up through the restaurant terrace and find the big, long tunnel next to the parking garage—this will deposit you in the middle of Amalfi.

From Atrani, you could theoretically continue up to **Ravello** (described later in this chapter). But be warned: Unless you're part mountain goat, you'll probably prefer catching the bus to Ravello from Amalfi town instead.

Sleeping in Amalfi Town

Sleeps are much better in Positano (nicer views) or Sorrento (lower prices), but if you're marooned in Amalfi, here are some options. Prices listed are for high season (roughly April-Oct), but can spike in August and drop in spring and fall. Hotels are tricky to find in this town's labyrinthine street plan; from Piazza Duomo, look carefully for big hotel signs to get started in the right direction.

$$ Hotel Floridiana, just off the main drag and five minutes by foot from the harbor, is only three short flights of steps up from the street. Though lacking views, the 13 rooms are neat and clean. The well-run hotel has a gorgeous, frescoed breakfast room and comes with free garage parking—very unusual here (standard Db-€130-140, superior Db-€15 more, extra bed-€30, air-con, elevator, closed Nov-March; pass the Duomo, take the next right through tiny arch—Salita Brancia—and go up 30 steps to Via Brancia 1; tel. 089-873-6373, www.hotelfloridiana.it, info@hotelfloridiana. it, Agnese).

$$ Residenza del Duca is a little seven-room B&B with ornate furnishings, up many flights of stairs in the heart of this touristy enclave (minuscule Sb-€50, Db-€130-160, 5 percent direct-booking discount with this book and cash, air-con, no views but glimpses of ocean through the rooftops; 25 yards uphill from Piazza Duomo, take the first left, go up stairs and follow signs, then go up more stairs—over 70 total—to Via Mastalo II Duca 3; free luggage service available April-Oct 9:00-20:00—call ahead, tel. 089-873-6365, www.residencedelduca.it, info@residencedelduca. it, Andrea).

$$ Hotel Lidomare's 18 rooms are decorated in traditional majolica tiles and rich antique furnishings just a few steps from the Duomo. While a bit long in the tooth, it's central and conscientiously run by the aptly named Camera ("Room") family (Db-€140, air-con, faces its own little square just up the stairs across from the Duomo stairs—veer left to Largo Piccolomini 9, tel. 089-871-332, www.lidomare.it, info@lidomare.it, Santolo and his sister Maria).

$$ Hotel Aurora is a tranquil, bright, and cheery respite from Amalfi crowds. It's at the base of the biggest pier, overlooking the harbor and pedestrian promenade—a scenic 10-minute waterfront stroll from the town center (non-view Db-€149, view Db-€169, superior view Db with terrace-€189, family apartments available, air-con, elevator, parking-€20/day, Piazzale dei Protonini, tel. 089-871-209, www.aurora-hotel.it, info@aurora-hotel.it).

$$ Hotel Centrale—with 17 rooms in a, yes, central location—is faded and overpriced. It's a last resort that's worth considering if you can score one of the eight rooms that have a stunning view of the cathedral. These cost the same, but come with some noise (Db-€140, air-con, Largo Piccolomini 1, tel. 089-872-608, www.amalfihotelcentrale.it, amalfihotelcentrale@msn.com).

Eating in Amalfi Town

Grabbing a Quick Lunch: To grab a fast bite, walk five minutes up the main drag; on the right, past the first archway, is **Pizza Express,** with honest €4-6 pies, calzones, and heated sandwiches to go (Mon-Sat 9:00-21:00, closed Sun, Via Capuano 46, mobile 339-581-2336). The **Cuoppo d'Amalfi** fried-fish stand at Piazza dei Doge (described below) is another good option; there's also a small **supermarket** facing that piazza, and another supermarket (Decò) is just off of the main drag (up an alley to the right near #34, at Via Dei Curiali 6). Both supermarkets close for a midafternoon break and all day Sunday.

On the Main Square, Piazza Duomo: Several pricey places face the cathedral steps. The best of the bunch is tucked just around the left side of the grand staircase, up a smaller flight of stairs: **Taverna degli Apostoli,** with colorful outdoor tables and cozy upstairs dining room in what was once an art gallery. The menu is brief but thoughtful, going beyond the old standbys, and everything is well-executed (€12-14 pastas, €12-18 *secondi,* daily 12:00-16:00 & 19:00-24:00, Supportico San Andrea 6, tel. 089-872-991). For dessert, the **Andrea Pansa** pastry shop and café, to the right as you face the cathedral steps, is the most venerable place in town—a good spot to try *sfogliatella* (the delicate pastry invented at a nearby monastery) and other desserts popular in southern Italy.

Near the Main Square, on Piazza dei Doge: If you walk straight ahead from the cathedral stairs, go up the little covered lane, and hook right at the fork, you'll pop out in atmospheric little Piazza dei Doge. Slightly less trampled and more neighborhood-feeling than Piazza Duomo, this has several decent (if forgettable) restaurants aimed squarely at pleasing tourists. The **Cuoppo d'Amalfi** fried-fish shop, on the right as you enter the square, fills cardboard cones with all manner of deep-fried sea life. **Bar La Piazzetta** has good prices at its tables right in the middle of the square. And tucked at the corner of the square leading to the port, **La Taverna di Masaniello** is a bit pricier, with good food.

Ravello

The Amalfi Coast's version of a hill town, Ravello sits atop a lofty perch 1,000 feet above the sea. For such a small town, it boasts great sightseeing (an interesting church and two villas with stunning gardens) and breathtaking views that have attracted celebrities for generations. Gore Vidal, Richard Wagner, D. H. Lawrence, M. C. Escher, Henry Wadsworth Longfellow, and Greta Garbo all have succumbed to Ravello's charms and called it home.

The town is like a lush and peaceful garden floating above it all. It seems there's nothing but tourists, cafés, stones, old villas-turned-luxury hotels, and grand views. It's one big place to convalesce.

Ravello can make for a half-day outing from Amalfi, or a full

AMALFI COAST

day from Positano with a stop in Amalfi. The views from the bus ride up and back are every bit as stunning as those along the coastal route.

Sights in Ravello

To see the sights listed here, start at the bus stop and walk through the tunnel to the main square, where you'll find the Villa Rufolo on the left, the church on the right, and the **TI** down the street past the church (TI open daily May-Oct 10:00-18:00, closes earlier off-season, 100 yards from the square—follow signs to Via Roma 18, tel. 089-857-096, www.ravellotime.it). Villa Cimbrone is a 10-minute walk from the square (follow the signs).

If you only have time for one villa, consider this: Villa Rufolo is easier to reach (facing the main square) and has a stunning terrace garden. Villa Cimbrone requires an up-and-down hike, but it's bigger and more rugged, and offers even grander views in both directions along the coast.

Piazza Duomo

The town's entry tunnel deposits you on the main square. Though Ravello is perfectly peaceful today, the watchtower of Villa Rufolo—which once kept an eye out for fires and invasions—is a reminder that it wasn't always postcards and *limoncello*. The facade of the cathedral is plain because the earlier, fancy west portal was destroyed in a 1364 earthquake. The front door is locked; to enter, you need to go through the museum on Viale Wagner, around the left side. The fine umbrella pines on the square provide a shady meeting place for strollers ending up here on the piazza. Opposite the church is a fine view of the terraced hillside and the community of Scala (which means "steps"—historically a way of life there). The terraces—supporting grapevines and lemon trees—mostly date from the 16th century. Viale Wagner climbs to the top of town for sea views and ruined villas that are now luxury hotels. The town is essentially traffic-free.

Duomo

Ravello's cathedral, overlooking the main square, feels stripped-down and Romanesque, with tastefully restrained decoration and a floor that slopes upward. The key features of this church are its 12th-century bronze doors (from Constantinople), with 54 Biblical scenes; the carved marble pulpit supported by six lions; and the chance to get a close-up look at the relic of holy blood (left of main altar). The geometric designs show Arabic influence. The humble cathedral museum, through which you'll enter, is two rooms of well-described carved marble that evoke the historical importance of the town.

Cost and Hours: €3 for the museum—which also gets you into the church, daily May-Oct 9:00-19:00, Nov-April 9:00-18:00, enter through museum (around left side of cathedral).

Villa Rufolo

The villa, built in the 13th-century ruins of a noble family's palace, presents wistful gardens among stony walls, with oh-my-God views. The Arabic/Norman gardens seem designed to frame commanding coastline vistas (you can enjoy the same view, without the entry fee, from the bus parking lot just below the villa). It's also one of the venues for Ravello's annual arts festival (July-Sept, www.ravellofestival.com) and music society performances (April-June and Sept-Oct, www.ravelloarts.org). Musicians perch on a bandstand on the edge of the cliff for a combination of wonderful music and dizzying views. Wagner visited here and was impressed enough to set the second act of his opera *Parsifal* in the villa's magical gardens. By all accounts, the concert on the cliff is a sublime experience.

Cost and Hours: €5, daily May-Sept 9:00-20:00, Oct-April 9:00 until sunset, may close earlier for concerts, tel. 089-857-621, www.villarufolo.it.

Visiting the Villa: From Piazza Duomo, you'll enter through the stout watchtower to buy your ticket, then walk through part of the sprawling villa ruins. Finally you'll pop out at a viewpoint overlooking the neatly geometrical garden terrace, which you're welcome to climb down and explore.

▲Villa Cimbrone

This villa provides another romantic garden, this one built upon the ruins of an old convent. Located at the opposite end of Ravello, it was created in the 20th century by Englishman William Beckett. His mansion is now a five-star hotel. It's a longish walk to the end of town, where you explore a bluff dreamily landscaped around the villa. At the far end, above a sublime café on the lawn, "the Terrace of Infinity" dangles high above the sea.

Cost and Hours: €7, daily 9:00-sunset, tel. 089-857-459, www.villacimbrone.com.

Getting There: Facing the cathedral on Piazza Duomo, exit the square to the right and follow signs. You'll climb up and down (and up and down) some stair-step lanes, enjoying a quieter side of Ravello, before reaching the villa at the point.

Visiting the Villa: Buy your ticket and pick up the free map/guide of the gardens. Across from the ticket booth, duck into the old monastery. Then pass the rose-garden terrace and head up the "main boulevard," which leads straight to the stunning Terrace of Infinity, with 360-degree views up and down the coast. If you have the interest and energy, loop back along the more rugged downhill slope (facing the adjacent town of Scala). Tiny lizards scurry underfoot, while mythological statues (Mercury's Seat, Temple of Bacchus, Eve's Grotto) strike their poses before a stunning and serene backdrop.

▲Hike to Amalfi Town from Villa Cimbrone

To walk downhill from Ravello's Villa Cimbrone to the town of Amalfi (a path for hardy hikers only—follow the TI's map), retrace your steps back toward town. Take the first left, which turns into a stepped path winding its way below the cliff. Pause here to look back up at the rock with a big white mansion—Villa La Rondinaia, where Gore Vidal lived for many years. Continue down the fairly steep path about 40 minutes to the town of Atrani, where several bars on the main square offer well-deserved refreshment. From here, it's about a 15-minute walk back to Amalfi.

Eating in Ravello

In Town: Several no-brainer, interchangeable restaurants face Piazza Duomo and line the surrounding streets. To enjoy this fine setting, just take your pick. You can also grab a takeaway lunch at one of the little groceries and sandwich shops that line Via Roma (between Piazza Duomo and the TI). Enjoy your meal at the panoramic benches at the far end of Piazza Duomo (facing the cathedral), or facing even better views just outside of town, near the bus stop and Ristorante Da Salvatore. (Picnicking isn't allowed inside the two villas.)

Just Outside of Town, with Stunning Views: **Ristorante Da Salvatore** serves a serious sit-down lunch that takes full advantage of the views that make a trip to Ravello worthwhile. Pino, the English-speaking owner of this formal restaurant, serves nicely presented, traditional Amalfi cuisine from a fun, if pricey, menu. Be adventurous when ordering and share dishes. Pato, the parakeet, is learning English (€13-18 pastas, €16-19 *secondi*, Tue-Sun 12:30-15:00 & 19:30-22:00, closed Mon, located where buses and taxis drop those visiting town, Via della Repubblica 2, tel. 089-857-227, reservations smart).

Ravello Connections

Ravello and the town of **Amalfi** are connected by a winding road and a bus. Coming from Amalfi town, buy your ticket at the bar on the waterfront, and ask where the bus stop is (normally by the statue on the waterfront, just to the statue's left as you face the water). In Ravello, line up early, since the buses are often crowded (at least every 40 minutes, 30-minute trip, €1.20, buy ticket in tobacco shop; catch bus 100 yards off main square, at other end of tunnel).

You can also reach Ravello from **Naples** via Salerno. Take the train from Naples to Salerno (2/hour, 35-60 minutes), and then go by bus or boat to Amalfi town, where you can catch the bus to Ravello described above. Salerno's TI has bus, ferry, and train schedules; see "Paestum Connections," later, for details.

Paestum

The ruins at Paestum (PASTE-oom) include one of the best collections of Greek temples anywhere—and certainly the most accessible to Western Europe. Serenely situated, Paestum is surrounded by fields and wildflowers. It also has a functional zone with a bus stop, train station, church, and a straggle of houses and cafés that you could barely call a village.

This town was founded as Poseidonia by Greeks in the sixth century B.C., and became a key stop on an important trade route. In the fifth century B.C., the Lucanians, a barbarous inland tribe, conquered Poseidonia and tried to adopt the cultured ways of the Greeks. By the time of the Romans, who took over in the third century B.C., the name Poseidonia had been simplified to Paestum. The final conquerors of Paestum, malaria-carrying mosquitoes, kept the site wonderfully deserted for nearly a thousand years. The temples were never buried—just ignored. Rediscovered in the 18th century, Paestum today offers the only well-preserved Greek ruins north of Sicily.

While most visitors do Paestum as a day trip, it's not a bad place to overnight. Accommodations offer great value, and though it's a bit far, you could use Paestum as a base for day trips to Naples or the Amalfi Coast. There's a beach nearby, and hotels can help arrange visits to local buffalo-milk dairies.

Tourist Information: There's a small TI window at the train station (daily 8:30-18:30) and a bigger one next to the Paestum Archaeological Museum (daily 9:00-13:00 & 15:00-17:00, tel. 0828-811-016, www.infopaestum.it).

AMALFI COAST

AMALFI COAST

GETTING TO PAESTUM

While Naples has direct connections to Paestum, from elsewhere you'll likely have to transfer in Salerno (see map). If you need to grab a bite while awaiting your train in Salerno, I've noted a few handy takeaway places on the map.

From Naples: The simplest way to reach Paestum is by direct **train** from Naples' Centrale Station (10/day, 1.5 hours). Buy tickets from the ticket windows or machines at the station (stamp before boarding). For a morning visit from Naples, it's wise to get an early start—especially in warm weather; check the schedule at stations or www.trenitalia.it.

From Amalfi or Positano: First, take either a bus or boat to Salerno, where you can pick up the **train** to Paestum on its way from Naples (30-40 minutes). Buy your train ticket at the ticket machines, ticket office, or the newsstand in the Salerno train station (stamp before boarding). Buses from Amalfi terminate at the Salerno train station, but if you arrive in Salerno from the Amalfi Coast by boat, you'll walk from the boat dock a few short blocks up to the train station (about 10 minutes, mostly level; see map).

If you're in a pinch—for example, there's often a midday lull in the train schedule—you could take **local CSTP bus #34** from Salerno to Paestum (about hourly, less on Sun, 1-hour trip). It seems convenient to the port (it departs from Piazza della Concordia—look for bus shelter between the big parking lot and the main road, no posted schedule), but you can't buy tickets nearby—the closest sales point is the tobacco shop a block in front of the train station. In Paestum, this bus drops you only slightly closer to the ruins than does the train.

From Sorrento: While it's technically possible to day-trip from Sorrento to Paestum by public transport (via Amalfi and Salerno), it makes for a very long day marred by worry about making connections back. Consider renting a car or hiring a taxi for the day. From Sorrento, Paestum is 60 miles and 3 hours via the coast (longer with summer traffic), but a smooth 2 hours by autostrada. To reach Paestum from Sorrento via the autostrada, drive toward Naples, catch the autostrada (direction: Salerno), skirt Salerno (direction: Reggio), exit at Battipaglia, and drive straight through the roundabout. Along the way, you'll see signs for *mozzarella di bufala*, cheese made from the milk of water buffalo. Try it here—it can't be any fresher.

ARRIVAL AT PAESTUM

If you arrive by train, cross under the tracks, exit the tiny station, and walk through the ancient city gate; the ruins are a 10-minute walk straight ahead, up a dusty road. When you hit the street with hotels and shops, turn right to find the museum and site entrance. Buses from Salerno stop near a corner of the ruins (at a little bar/café). There's no official baggage storage at the train station or museum. If you're desperate, you can try nicely asking one of the bars along the main road (they may want a small payment).

PLANNING YOUR TIME

Allow two hours to see the ruins and the museum. Which one you see first depends on your interest and the heat. You'll enjoy the best light and smallest crowds late in the day.

ORIENTATION TO PAESTUM

Cost: €10, includes site and museum.

Hours: Museum open daily 8:30-19:30 (last ticket sold at 18:45), except closed the first and third Mon of each month. Site open daily 8:45 to one hour before sunset (as late as 19:30 June-July, as early as 15:30 in mid-Dec, last site ticket sold one hour before closing).

Getting In: The site and museum have separate entrances. The museum, just outside the ruins, is in a cluster with the TI and

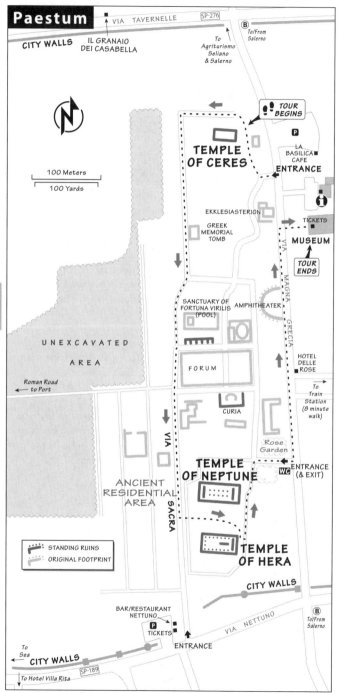

a small early-Christian basilica. Most visitors buy tickets at the museum and use the entrance across the street, but another ticket office and entrance is near the recommended Ristorante Nettuno (at the south end of the site). On days when the museum is closed, you have to buy tickets at the site entrances.

Information: While there are scant descriptions at the site itself, the self-guided tours in this chapter provide all the information you need for both the site and the museum. The museum bookshop sells several mediocre guidebooks. Dull €6 audioguides are available to rent at the museum. The €1.50 booklet, sold at the ticket desk, gives only general information and is more souvenir than guide. Info tel. 0828-811-023.

Local Guide: Silvia Braggio is a good guide who gives a fine two-hour walk of the site and museum (special rate with this book-€100, arrange in advance, mobile 347-643-2307, www.silviaguide.it, silvia@silviaguide.it). She also offers walking tours of Pompeii and Herculaneum.

Eating: Several cafés and bars cluster around the museum (all open long hours daily in summer); **La Basilica Café,** facing a pretty little garden between the parking lot and TI, is the most straightforward and reasonable option, with good €5-8 pizzas and other lunch fare (Via Magna Grecia 881, tel. 0828-811-301). **Ristorante Nettuno,** with quality food and good temple views, is at the south entrance to the site. They have a fine little glassed-in café facing the ruins (affordable light food, including a fixed-price lunch) and a dressier, more expensive restaurant across the path.

SELF-GUIDED TOURS
Paestum Archaeological Site

This tour starts at the entrance by the museum, visits the Temple of Ceres, goes through the center of the Roman town past the Greek Memorial Tomb, circles around the other two Greek temples, and then leaves the site to walk down the modern road to the Ekklesiasterion (which faces the museum).

Background: While Paestum is famous for its marvelous Greek temples, most of the structures you see are Roman. Five elements of Greek Paestum survive: three misnamed temples, a memorial tomb, and a circular meeting place (the Ekklesiasterion). The rest, including the wall that defines the site, is Roman.

Paestum was once a seaport (the ocean is now about a mile away—the wall in the distance, which stretches about three miles, is about halfway to today's coastline). Only about a fifth of the site has been excavated. The Greek city, which archaeologists figure had a population of about 13,000, was first conquered by Lucanians (distant relatives of the Romans, who spoke a language related to Latin), and then by the Romans (who completely made it over and built the wall you see today).

The remaining Greek structures survive because the Romans were superstitious—they respected sacred areas and didn't mess with temples and tombs. While most old Christian churches are built upon Roman temples (it tends to be what people do when they conquer another culture), no Roman temple is built upon a Greek temple. Romans appreciated how religion could function as the opiate of the masses. As long as people paid their taxes and obeyed the emperor's dictates, the practical Romans had no problem with any religion. The three Greek temples that you'll see here today have stood for about 2,500 years.

• *Buy your ticket at the museum, then head to the right to find the site's north entrance. Once inside, stand in front of the...*

Temple of Ceres: All three Paestum temples have inaccurate names, coined by 19th-century archaeologists who based their "discoveries" on wishful think-

ing. (While the Romans made things easy by leaving lots of inscriptions, the Greeks did not.) Those 1800s archaeologists wanted this temple to be devoted to Ceres, the goddess of agriculture. However, all the little votive statues found later, when modern archaeologists dug here, instead depicted a woman with a big helmet: Athena, goddess of wisdom and war. (The Greeks' female war goddess was also the goddess of wisdom—thinking...strategy...female. The Romans' masculine war god was Mars—just fighting.) Each temple is part of a sanctuary—an open, sacred space around the temple. Because regular people couldn't go into the temple, the altar logically stood outside.

The Temple of Ceres dates from 500 B.C. It's made of locally quarried limestone blocks. Good roads and shipping didn't come along until the Romans, so the Greeks' buildings were limited to local materials. The wooden roof is long gone. Like the other two temples, this one was once painted white, black, and red, and has an east-west orientation—facing the rising sun. This temple's *cella* (interior room) is gone, cleared out when it was used as a Christian church in the sixth century. In medieval times, Normans scavenged stones from here; chunks of these temples can be found in Amalfi's cathedral.

Walk around to the back side of the Temple of Ceres. The capitals broke in a modern earthquake, so a steel bar provides necessary support. Each of the Paestum temples is Doric style—with three stairs, columns without a base, and shafts that narrow at the top to a simple capital of a round then a square block. While there were no carved reliefs, colorful frescoes once decorated the pediments.

As you walk away, look back at the temple. Traditionally, Greeks would build a sanctuary of Athena on a city's highest spot (like the Parthenon in Athens, on the Acropolis). Paestum had no hill, so the Greeks created a mound. The hill was more impressive in its time because the level of the Greek city was substantially lower than the Roman pavement stones you'll walk on today.

• *Continue all the way past the temple, follow the path down, and turn left to walk on the paving stones of Via Sacra toward the other Greek temples. After about 100 yards, to the left of the road, you'll see a little half-buried house with a tiled roof.*

Greek Memorial Tomb (Heroon): This tomb (from 500 B.C.) also survived because the Romans respected religious buildings. But the tomb was most inconveniently located, right in the middle of their growing city. So the practical Romans built a perimeter wall around it (visible today), added a fine tiled roof, and then buried the tomb.

There's a mystery here. Greeks generally buried their dead outside the city (as did Romans)—there are over a thousand ancient tombs outside Paestum's walls—yet this tomb was parked smack-dab in the center of town. When it was uncovered in 1952, no bodies were found inside. The tomb instead held nine perfectly preserved vases (now in the museum). Archaeologists aren't sure of the tomb's purpose. Perhaps it was a memorial dedicated to some great hero (like a city founder). Or perhaps it was a memorial to those lost when a neighboring community had to evacuate and settle as refugees here.

• *Continue walking down Via Sacra, the main drag of...*

Roman Paestum: Roman towns were garrison towns: rectangular with a grid street plan and two main streets cutting north-south and east-west, dividing the town into four equal sections. They were built by military engineers with a no-nonsense standard design. New excavations (on the left) have uncovered Roman-era lead piping. City administration buildings were on the left, and residential buildings were on the right.

Shortly after the road turns into a dirt path, you'll come to a big **Roman pool** (on the left) that archaeologists believe was a sanctuary dedicated to Fortuna Virilis, goddess of luck and fertility. The strange stones likely supported a wooden platform for priests and statues of gods. Imagine young women walking down the ramp at the far end and through the pool, hoping to conceive a child.

The next big square on the left was the **Roman forum** and an-

AMALFI COAST

cient Paestum's main intersection. The road on the right led direct-ly (and very practically) to the port. It made sense to have a direct connection to move freight between the sea and the center of town.

Until 2007, the vast field of ruins on the right (between the forum and the next temple) was covered in vegetation. It's since been cleared and cleaned of harmful lichen, which produce acids that dissolve limestone. Study the rocks: Yellow lichen is alive, black is dead. Even the great temples of Paestum were covered in this destructive lichen until 2000, when a two-year-long project cleaned them for the first time.

• *Ahead on the left are the so-called...*

Temples of Neptune and Hera: The **Temple of Neptune** dates from 450 B.C. and employs the Greek ar-chitectural trick where the base line is curved up just a tad, to overcome the illusion of sagging caused by a straight base. The Athenians built their Par-thenon (with a similar bowed-up base line) just 30 years after this. Many think this temple could have been their inspiration.

The adjacent **Temple of Hera,** dating from 550 B.C., is the old-est of Paestum's three temples and one of the oldest Greek temples still standing anywhere. Notice the change 100 years makes in the architectural styles: Ar-chaic Doric in 550 B.C. versus Classic Doric in 450 B.C.

Archaeologists now be-lieve the "Temple of Neptune" was actually devoted to a dif-ferent god. Votive statues uncovered here suggest that Hera was the focus (perhaps this was a new and improved version of the adjacent, simpler, and older Temple of Hera). Or perhaps it was a temple to Zeus, Hera's husband, to honor the couple together.

Together, the two temples formed a single huge sanctuary with altars on the far (east) side. Walk between the temples, then hook right to get a good look at the front of the Temple of Hera. Notice how overbuilt this temple appears. Its columns and capi-tals are closer together than necessary, as if the builders lacked confidence in their ability to span the distance between supports. Square pillars mark the corners of the *cella* inside. Temples with an odd number of columns (here, nine) had a single colonnade cross-ing in the center inside to support the wooden roof. More modern temples (such as the Temple of Neptune) had six columns, with two colonnades passing through the *cella*. This left a line of vision open through the middle so that worshippers could see the big statue of the god.

By the way, in 1943, Allied paratroopers dropped in near here during the famous "Landing of Salerno," when the Allies (who had already taken Sicily) invaded mainland Italy. Paestum was part of their first beachhead. The Temple of Hera served as an Allied military tent hospital. From here, the Allies pushed back the Nazis, marching to Naples, Cassino, and finally to Rome.

• *Leave the site (using the exit straight ahead from the Temple of Neptune and a bit to the left) and turn left on the modern road...*

Via Magna Grecia: The king of Naples had this Naples-to-Paestum road built in 1829 to inspire his people with ancient temples. While he was modern in his appreciation of antiquity, his road project destroyed a swath of the ancient city, as you'll see as you pass by half of the small amphitheater.

• *Just past the amphitheater, you'll find the...*

Ekklesiasterion: Immediately across the street from the museum is what looks like a sunken circular theater. This rare bit of ancient Greek ruins was the Ekklesiasterion, a meeting place where the Greeks would get together to discuss things and vote. Archaeologists believe that the agora (market) would also have been located here.

• *Across the street is the...*

Paestum Archaeological Museum

Paestum's museum offers the rare opportunity to see artifacts—dating from prehistoric to Greek to Roman times—at the site where they were discovered. These beautifully crafted works (with good English descriptions throughout) help bring Paestum to life. Not everything you see here is from Paestum, though, as the museum also collects artifacts from other nearby sites.

Before stepping into the museum, notice the proud fascist architecture. Though the building dates from 1954, it was designed in 1938. It seems to command that you *will* enjoy this history lesson.

The exhibit is on several levels. You'll find mostly Greek pieces on the ground floor (artifacts from the Temple of Hera in front, frescoes from tombs in the back), Paleolithic to Iron Age artifacts on the mezzanine level, and Roman art on the top floor (statues, busts, and inscriptions dating from the time of the Roman occupation). While Roman art is not unique to Paestum, the Greek collection is—so that's what you should focus on. Here are the highlights:

Temple Reliefs: The museum's first room is designed like a Greek temple, with an inner *cella* that is used for temporary exhibitions. The large carvings overhead that wrap around this inner sanctum once adorned a sanctuary of the goddess Hera (wife of

Zeus) five miles away. This sanctuary, called Heraion del Sele, was discovered and excavated in 1934. Some of the carvings show scenes from the life of Hercules.

• *Along the back wall of this room, find the glass case holding nine perfectly preserved...*

Vases: One ceramic and eight bronze, with artistic handles, these vases were found in Paestum's Greek Memorial Tomb (if these vases are off-view for restoration, look for the similar bronze vases upstairs, at the end of this tour). Greek bronzes are rare because Romans often melted them down to make armor. These were discovered in 1952, filled with still-liquid honey and sealed with beeswax. The honey (as you can see in the display cases below) has since crystallized. Honey was a standard part of a funeral because, to ancient Greeks, honey symbolized immortality...it lasts forever.

• *Enter the room at the far end of the main hall, filled with ancient Greek...*

Votive Offerings: These were dug up at Heraion del Sele (not at Paestum). Such offerings are a huge help to modern archaeologists, since the figures worshippers brought to a temple are clues as to which god the temple honored. These votives depict a woman with a crown on a throne—clearly Hera. The clay votives were simple, affordable, and accessible to regular people.

• *Now enter the large room (broken up by pillars and interior walls) that holds...*

Relics from the Temples at Paestum: This room displays smaller pieces. Displays (mostly in Italian) tell in which temple each relic was found. The Temple of Ceres is often referred to as the Temple of Athena or as the northern *(settentrionale)* sanctuary. The Temples of Neptune and Hera are spoken of as the southern *(meridionale)* sanctuaries. Before exploring the collection, notice the display case near the entrance with the **huge book** turned to a page with a fine drawing by the Italian artist Giovanni Piranesi, showing his visit to Paestum in 1777.

Across the room, look for the short fragment of a **frieze** with lion heads. Paestum's three temples were once adorned with decorations, such as these ornamental spouts that spurted rainwater out of lions' mouths. Notice the bits of the surviving black, red, and white paint. Reconstructions on the adjacent wall show archaeologists' best guesses as to how the original decorations might have looked.

Farther into the room, you can't miss the display case of a statue's **torso** emblazoned with swastikas—a reminder that this symbol (carrying completely different meanings) predated Hitler by millennia.

In a glass case nearby, find the seated statue of **Zeus.** This painted clay Zeus dates from 520 B.C. The king of the gods was so lusty with his antics, he's still smirking.

• *Look out the museum's back window for a good, if distant...*

View of Paestum's Walls: The walls of ancient Paestum reach halfway to the mountain—a reminder that most of the site is still private property and yet to be excavated. The town up on the mountainside is Capaccio, established in the eighth century when inhabitants of the original city of Paestum were driven out by malaria and the city was abandoned.

• *Walk along the corridor at the back of the museum, which shows...*

Objects from Tombs: More than 1,000 tombs have been identified outside of the ancient city's wall. About 100 were found decorated with frescoes or containing objects such as these.

• *At the far end of the corridor, turn left to see...*

The Tomb of the Diver: This is the museum's treasure and the most precious Paestum find. Dating from 480 B.C., it's not only the

sole ancient Greek tomb fresco in the museum—it's the only one ever found in southern Italy. Discovered in 1968, it has five frescoed slabs (four sides and a lid; the bottom wasn't decorated). The Greeks saw death as a passage: diving from mortality into immortality...into an unknown world. Archaeologists believe that the pillars shown on the fresco represent the Pillars of Hercules at Gibraltar, which in ancient times defined the known world. The ocean beyond the Mediterranean was the great unknown...like the afterlife. The Greek banquet makes it clear that this was an aristocratic man.

• *After the Tomb of the Diver, the next room displays...*

Lucanian Tomb Frescoes: The many other painted slabs in the museum date from a later time, around 350 B.C., when Paestum fell under Lucanian rule. These frescoes are cruder than their earlier Greek counterpart. The people who conquered the Greeks tried to appropriate their art and style, but they lacked the Greeks' distinctive light touch. Still, these offer fascinating glimpses into ancient life here at Paestum.

• *Beyond this room, you'll find yourself back at the entrance. Before you leave, go up the stairs by the bookshop for a glimpse at the mezzanine level, which focuses on prehistoric archaeology. The exhibit here has much better English translations than the ground floor. At the very least, near the end of the first hall, check out the...*

Film Footage from WWII: A 10-minute continuous film loop, subtitled in English, tells the story of Allied soldiers' encounters with the ruins in 1943. You'll see footage of soldiers hanging up their laundry and shaving in the temples, which they actually safeguarded well. Part of the film focuses on excavations directed by a British archaeologist who was attached to the invading forces.

• *The back wall of the mezzanine displays* **bronze vases**, *mostly from Gaudo, a half-mile from Paestum. If the vases downstairs are missing, here's your chance to see some rare surviving examples of this common Greek vessel.*

SLEEPING IN PAESTUM

Paestum at night, with views of the floodlit ruins, is magic. Accommodations here offer great value. You can sleep in a mansion for the same price you'd pay for a closet in Positano. The prices listed are for high season (which rise further in Aug). All have free parking.

$ Il Granaio dei Casabella, a converted old granary with 14 attractive, reasonably priced rooms, is a 10-minute walk from the ruins. It has a beautiful garden and pretty common areas, and four rooms have temple views (Sb-€70, Db-€90, Tb-€110, Qb-€125, "economy" room on second floor with no elevator-€10 less, about €10 more in Aug, 10 percent discount if you mention Rick Steves when you book direct, air-con, just west of the bus stop closest to Salerno at Via Tavernelle 84, tel. 0828-721-014, www.ilgranaiodeicasabella.com, info@ilgranaiodeicasabella.com, hospitable Celardo family).

$ Hotel Villa Rita is a tidy, quiet country hotel set on two acres within walking distance of the beach and the temples. It has 22 rooms, a kid-friendly swimming pool, and attractive grounds with grassy lawns and a little soccer field (Sb-€70, Db-€90-100, €130 in Aug, third bed-€15, lunch or dinner-€20, 10 percent discount with this book and cash in 2016—can't be combined with other offers, air-con, closed Nov-March, Via Nettuno 9, tel. 0828-811-081, www.hotelvillarita.it, info@hotelvillarita.it, Luigi). The hotel is a 10-minute walk west of the Hera entrance and public bus stop, and a 20-minute walk from the train station (they can usually pick you up, if you're arriving with luggage).

$ Hotel delle Rose, with 10 small, basic rooms with minuscule bathrooms, is near the Neptune entrance on the street bordering the ruins. It's an acceptable choice for those on a budget and is also the option closest to the ruins and the train station (Sb-€35, Db-€60, Tb-€70, Qb-€85, these prices in 2016 if you mention this book and reserve directly with the hotel, air-con, Via Magna Grecia 943, tel. 0828-199-0692, www.hotelristorantedellerose.com, info@hotelristorantedellerose.com, Luigi).

Near Paestum

$ Agriturismo Seliano is a great option for drivers, with plush public spaces, a pool, and 14 grand, spacious rooms on a peaceful, once-elegant farm estate that's been in the same family for 300 years (Db-€70-90, €110 in Aug, air-con, closed Nov-March; one mile north of ruins on main road—Via Magna Grecia—a small *Azienda Agrituristica Seliano* sign directs you down long dirt drive-way; Via Seliano, tel. 0828-723-634, www.agriturismoseliano. it, seliano@agriturismoseliano.it). They serve a fine lunch or din-ner with produce fresh from the garden (€20 for guests, €25 for nonguests, price includes drinks) and can also organize cooking classes. The place is run by Cecilia—an English-speaking baron-ess—and her family, including about a dozen dogs.

PAESTUM CONNECTIONS

By Train: Ten slow, milk-run trains a day head to Salerno (30-40 minutes) and Naples (1.5 hours). In Salerno, you can change for the bus to Amalfi, or walk down to the harbor to catch an Amalfi- or Positano-bound boat. You can buy train tickets at machines in the (unstaffed) Paestum station.

   By Bus to Salerno: Buses depart from Paestum to Salerno roughly every hour (less on Sun; one-hour trip). Buy a ticket from one of the bars in Paestum, then go to either of the intersections that flank the ruins, flag down any northbound bus, and ask, "Salerno?" From Salerno, you can continue on to Amalfi or Posi-tano by boat, or walk up to the train station to catch an Amalfi-bound SITA bus or a train.

AMALFI COAST

PRACTICALITIES

This section covers just the basics on traveling in Italy (for much more information, see *Rick Steves Italy*). You'll find free advice on specific topics at www.ricksteves.com/tips.

MONEY

Italy uses the euro currency: 1 euro (€) = about $1.10. To convert prices in euros to dollars, add about 10 percent: €20 = about $22, €50 = about $55. (Check www.oanda.com for the latest exchange rates.)

The standard way for travelers to get euros is to withdraw money from ATMs (which locals call a *bancomat*) using a debit or credit card, ideally with a Visa or MasterCard logo. Before departing, call your bank or credit-card company: Confirm that your card(s) will work overseas, ask about international transaction fees, and alert them that you'll be making withdrawals in Europe. Also ask for the PIN number for your credit card in case it'll help you use Europe's "chip-and-PIN" payment machines (see below); allow time for your bank to mail your PIN to you. To keep your valuables safe while traveling, wear a money belt.

Dealing with "Chip and PIN": Much of Europe (including Italy) is adopting a "chip-and-PIN" system for credit cards, and some merchants rely on it exclusively. European chip-and-PIN cards are embedded with an electronic chip, in addition to the magnetic stripe used on our American-style cards. This means that your credit (and debit) card might not work at payment machines, such as those at train and subway stations, toll roads, parking garages, luggage lockers, and gas pumps. Major US banks are beginning to offer credit cards with chips, but many of these are chip-and-signature cards, for which your signature (not your PIN) verifies your identity. In Europe, these cards should work for live transactions and at most payment machines, but probably won't work for offline transactions such as at unattended gas pumps. If a payment machine won't take your card, look for a machine that takes cash or see if there's a cashier nearby who can manually process your transaction. Often the easiest solution is to pay for your purchases with cash you've withdrawn from an ATM using your debit card (Europe's ATMs still accept magnetic-stripe cards).

Dynamic Currency Conversion: If merchants or hoteliers offer to convert your purchase price into dollars (called dynamic currency conversion, or DCC), refuse this "service." You'll pay more in fees for the expensive convenience of seeing your charge in dollars. If an ATM offers to "lock in" or "guarantee" your conversion rate, choose "proceed without conversion." Other prompts might state, "You can be charged in dollars: Press YES for dollars, NO for euros." Always choose the local currency.

STAYING CONNECTED

Smart travelers call ahead or go online to double-check tourist information, learn the latest on sights (special events, tour schedules, and so on), book tickets and tours, make reservations, reconfirm hotels, and research transportation connections.

To call Italy from the US or Canada: Dial 011-39 and then the local number. (The 011 is our international access code, and 39 is Italy's country code.)

To call Italy from a European country: Dial 00-39 followed by the local number. (The 00 is Europe's international access code.)

To call within Italy: Just dial the local number.

To call from Italy to another country: Dial 00 followed by the country code (for example, 1 for the US or Canada), then the area code and number. If you're calling European countries whose phone numbers begin with 0, you'll usually omit that 0 when you dial.

Tips: Traveling with a mobile phone—whether an American one that works in Italy, or a European one you buy when you arrive—is handy, but can be pricey. Consider getting an international plan; most providers offer a global calling plan that cuts the per-minute cost of phone calls and texts, and a flat-fee data plan.

Use Wi-Fi whenever possible. Most hotels and many cafés offer free Wi-Fi, and you'll likely also find it at tourist information offices, major museums, and public-transit hubs. With Wi-Fi you can use your smartphone to make free or inexpensive domestic and international calls by taking advantage of a calling app such as Skype, FaceTime, or Google+ Hangouts. When you can't find Wi-Fi, you can use your cellular network to connect to the Internet, text, or make voice calls. When you're done, avoid further charges by manually switching off "data roaming" or "cellular data."

It's possible to stay connected without a mobile phone. To make cheap international calls from any phone (even your hotel-room

PRACTICALITIES

From:	rick@ricksteves.com
Sent:	Today
To:	info@hotelcentral.com
Subject:	Reservation request for 19-22 July

Dear Hotel Central,

I would like to reserve a double room for 2 people for 3 nights, arriving 19 July and departing 22 July. If possible, I would like a quiet room with a bathroom inside the room.

Please let me know if you have a room available and the price.

Thank you!
Rick Steves

phone), you can buy an international phone card in Italy. These work with a scratch-to-reveal PIN code, allow you to call home to the US for pennies a minute, and also work for domestic calls. Calling from your hotel-room phone without using an international phone card is usually expensive. Though they are disappearing in Italy, you can still find public pay phones in post offices and train stations. For more on phoning, see www.ricksteves.com/phoning.

MAKING HOTEL RESERVATIONS

I recommend reserving rooms in advance, particularly during peak season. For the best rates, book directly with the hotel using their official website (not a booking agency's site). If there's no secure reservation form, or for complicated requests, send an email with the following information: number and type of rooms; number of nights; arrival date; departure date; and any special requests. (For a sample email, see the sidebar.) Use the European style for writing dates: day/month/year. Hoteliers typically ask for your credit-card number as a deposit.

Some hotels are willing to deal to attract guests—try emailing several to ask their best price. In general, hotel prices can soften if you do any of the following: offer to pay cash, stay at least three nights, or travel off-season. You can also try asking for a cheaper room or a discount.

While most taxes are included in the price, a variable city tax of €1.50-5/person per night is often added to hotel bills in Italy (and is not included in the prices in this book). Some hoteliers will ask to collect the city tax in cash to make their bookkeeping and accounting simpler.

EATING

Italy offers a wide array of eateries. A *ristorante* is a formal restaurant, while a *trattoria* or *osteria* is usually more traditional and simpler (but can still be pricey). Italian "bars" are not taverns, but small cafés selling sandwiches, coffee, and other drinks. An *enoteca* is a wine bar with snacks and light meals. Take-away food from pizza shops and delis (*rosticcería*) makes an easy picnic.

Italians eat dinner a bit later than we do; better restaurants start serving around 19:00. A full meal consists of an appetizer (antipasto), a first course (*primo piatto*, pasta, rice, or soup), and a second course (*secondo piatto*, expensive meat and fish/seafood dishes). Vegetables (*verdure*) may come with the *secondo*, but more often must be ordered separately as a side dish (*contorno*). Desserts (*dolci*) can be very tempting. The euros can add up in a hurry, but you don't have to order each course. My approach is to mix antipasti and *primi piatti* family-style with my dinner partners (skipping *secondi*). Or, for a basic value, look for a *menù del giorno*, a three- or four-course, fixed-price meal deal (avoid the cheapest ones, often called a *menù turistico*).

Good service is relaxed (slow to an American). You won't get the bill until you ask for it: *"Il conto?"* Most restaurants include a service charge in their prices (check the menu for *servizio incluso*— generally around 10 percent). You can add on a tip, if you choose, by including a euro or two for each person in your party. If you order at a counter rather than from waitstaff, there's no need to tip. Many (but not all) restaurants in Italy add a cover charge *(coperto)* of €1-3.50 per person to your bill.

At bars and cafés, getting a drink while standing at the bar (*banco)* is cheaper than drinking it at a table *(tavolo)* or sitting outside *(terrazza)*. This tiered pricing system is clearly posted on the wall. Sometimes you'll pay at a cash register, then take the receipt to another counter to claim your drink.

TRANSPORTATION

By Train: In Italy, most travelers find it's cheapest simply to buy train tickets as they go. To see if a railpass could save you money, check www.ricksteves.com/rail. To research train schedules, visit Germany's excellent all-Europe website, www.bahn.com, or Italy's www.trenitalia.com. A private company called Italo also runs fast trains on major routes in Italy; see www.italotreno.it.

You can buy tickets at train stations (at the ticket window or at machines with English instructions) or from travel agencies. Before boarding the train, you must validate your train documents by stamping them in the machine near the platform (usually marked *convalida biglietti* or *vidimazione*). Strikes *(sciopero)* are common and generally announced in advance (but a few sporadic trains still run—ask around).

By Car: It's cheaper to arrange most car rentals from the US. For tips on your insurance options, see www.ricksteves.com/

cdw, and for route planning, consult www.viamichelin.com. Theft insurance is mandatory in Italy ($15-20/day). In Italy, most car-rental companies' rates automatically include Collision Damage Waiver (CDW) coverage. Even if you try to decline CDW when you reserve your Italian car, you may find when you show up at the counter that you must buy it after all.

Bring your driver's license. You're also technically required to have an International Driving Permit (sold at your local AAA office for $15 plus the cost of two passport-type photos; see www.aaa.com).

Italy's superhighway *(autostrada)* system is slick and speedy, but you'll pay a toll. Be warned that car traffic is restricted in many city centers—don't drive or park in any area that has a sign reading *Zona Traffico Limitato* (ZTL, often shown above a red circle)...or you might be mailed a ticket later.

Italians love to tailgate; otherwise, local road etiquette is similar to that in the US. Ask your car-rental company for details, or check the US State Department website (www.travel.state.gov, click on "International Travel," then specify your country of choice and click "Traffic Safety and Road Conditions").

A car is a worthless headache in cities—park it safely (get tips from your hotelier). As break-ins are common, be sure all of your valuables are out of sight and locked in the trunk, or even better, with you or in your hotel room.

HELPFUL HINTS

Emergency Help: For English-speaking **police** help, dial 113. To summon an **ambulance**, call 118. For passport problems, call the **US Embassy** (in Rome, 24-hour line—tel. 06-46741) or **US Consulates** (Milan—tel. 02-290-351, Florence—tel. 055-266-951, Naples—tel. 081-583-8111); or the **Canadian Embassy** (in Rome, tel. 06-854-442-911). If you have a minor illness, do as the locals do and go to a pharmacist for advice. Or ask at your hotel for help—they'll know of the nearest medical and emergency services. For other concerns, get advice from your hotelier.

Theft or Loss: Italy has particularly hardworking pickpockets—wear a money belt. Assume beggars are pickpockets and any scuffle is simply a distraction by a team of thieves. If you stop for any commotion or show, put your hands in your pockets before someone else does.

To replace a passport, you'll need to go in person to an embassy or consulate (see above). Cancel and replace your credit and debit cards by calling these 24-hour US numbers collect: Visa—tel. 303/967-1096, MasterCard—tel. 636/722-7111, American Express—tel. 336/393-1111. In Italy, to make a collect call to the US, dial 800-172-444; press zero or stay on the line for an operator.

File a police report either on the spot or within a day or two; you'll need it to submit an insurance claim for lost or stolen railpasses or electronics, and it can help with replacing your passport or credit and debit cards. Precautionary measures can minimize the effects of loss—back up your digital photos and other files frequently. For more information, see www.ricksteves.com/help.

Time: Italy uses the 24-hour clock. It's the same through 12:00 noon, then keep going: 13:00, 14:00, and so on. Italy, like most of continental Europe, is six/nine hours ahead of the East/West Coasts of the US.

Business Hours: Many businesses have now adopted the government's recommended 8:00 to 14:00 workday (although in tourist areas, shops are open longer). Still, expect small towns and villages to be more or less shut tight during the midafternoon. Stores are also usually closed on Sunday, and often on Monday.

Sights: Opening and closing hours of sights can change unexpectedly; confirm the latest times with the local tourist information office or its website. Some major churches enforce a modest dress code (no bare shoulders or shorts) for everyone, even children.

Holidays and Festivals: Italy celebrates many holidays, which can close sights and attract crowds (book hotel rooms ahead). For information on holidays and festivals, check Italy's website: www.italia.it. For a simple list showing major—though not all—events, see www.ricksteves.com/festivals.

Numbers and Stumblers: What Americans call the second floor of a building is the first floor in Europe. Europeans write dates as day/month/year, so Christmas 2016 is 25/12/16. Commas are decimal points and vice versa—a dollar and a half is 1,50, and there are 5.280 feet in a mile. Italy uses the metric system: A kilogram is 2.2 pounds; a liter is about a quart; and a kilometer is six-tenths of a mile.

RESOURCES FROM RICK STEVES

This Snapshot guide is excerpted from my latest edition of *Rick Steves Italy*, which is one of more than 30 titles in my series of guidebooks on European travel. I also produce a public television series, *Rick Steves' Europe*, and a public radio show, *Travel with Rick Steves*. My website, www.ricksteves.com, offers free travel information, a forum for travelers' comments, guidebook updates, my travel blog, an online travel store, and information on European railpasses and our tours of Europe. If you're bringing a mobile device on your trip, you can download my free Rick Steves Audio Europe app, featuring podcasts of my radio shows, audio tours of major sights in Europe, and travel interviews about Italy. You can get Rick Steves Audio Europe via Apple's App Store, Google Play, or the Amazon Appstore. For more information, see www.

ricksteves.com/audioeurope. You can also follow me on Facebook and Twitter.

ADDITIONAL RESOURCES
Tourist Information: www.italia.it
Passports and Red Tape: www.travel.state.gov
Packing List: www.ricksteves.com/packing
Travel Insurance: www.ricksteves.com/insurance
Cheap Flights: www.kayak.com
Airplane Carry-on Restrictions: www.tsa.gov
Updates for This Book: www.ricksteves.com/update

How Was Your Trip?
If you'd like to share your tips, concerns, and discoveries after using this book, please fill out the survey at www.ricksteves.com/feedback. Thanks in advance—it helps a lot.

Italian Survival Phrases

English	Italian	Pronunciation
Good day.	*Buon giorno.*	bwohn **jor**-noh
Do you speak English?	*Parla inglese?*	**par**-lah een-**glay**-zay
Yes. / No.	*Sì. / No.*	see / noh
I (don't) understand.	*(Non) capisco.*	(nohn) kah-**pees**-koh
Please.	*Per favore.*	pehr fah-**voh**-ray
Thank you.	*Grazie.*	**graht**-seeay
You're welcome.	*Prego.*	**pray**-go
I'm sorry.	*Mi dispiace.*	mee dee-spee**ah**-chay
Excuse me.	*Mi scusi.*	mee **skoo**-zee
(No) problem.	*(Non) c'è un problema.*	(nohn) cheh oon proh-**blay**-mah
Good.	*Va bene.*	vah **behn**-ay
Goodbye.	*Arrivederci.*	ah-ree-vay-**dehr**-chee
one / two	*uno / due*	**oo**-noh / **doo**-ay
three / four	*tre / quattro*	tray / **kwah**-troh
five / six	*cinque / sei*	**cheeng**-kway / **seh**ee
seven / eight	*sette / otto*	**seht**-tay / **ot**-toh
nine / ten	*nove / dieci*	**nov**-ay / dee**eay**-chee
How much is it?	*Quanto costa?*	**kwahn**-toh **kos**-tah
Write it?	*Me lo scrive?*	may loh **skree**-vay
Is it free?	*È gratis?*	eh **grah**-tees
Is it included?	*È incluso?*	eh een-**kloo**-zoh
Where can I buy / find...?	*Dove posso comprare / trovare...?*	**doh**-vay **pos**-soh kohm-**prah**-ray / troh-**vah**-ray
I'd like / We'd like...	*Vorrei / Vorremmo...*	vor-**reh**ee / vor-**ray**-moh
...a room.	*...una camera.*	**oo**-nah **kah**-meh-rah
...a ticket to ____.	*...un biglietto per ____.*	oon beel-**yeht**-toh pehr
Is it possible?	*È possibile?*	eh poh-**see**-bee-lay
Where is...?	*Dov'è...?*	**doh**-veh
...the train station	*...la stazione*	lah staht-see**oh**-nay
...the bus station	*...la stazione degli autobus*	lah staht-see**oh**-nay **dayl**-yee **ow**-toh-boos
...tourist information	*...informazioni per turisti*	een-for-maht-see**oh**-nee pehr too-**ree**-stee
...the toilet	*...la toilette*	lah twah-**leht**-tay
men	*uomini, signori*	**woh**-mee-nee, seen-**yoh**-ree
women	*donne, signore*	**don**-nay, seen-**yoh**-ray
left / right	*sinistra / destra*	see-**nee**-strah / **dehs**-trah
straight	*sempre diritto*	**sehm**-pray dee-**ree**-toh
When do you open / close?	*A che ora aprite / chiudete?*	ah kay **oh**-rah ah-**pree**-tay / keeoo-**day**-tay
At what time?	*A che ora?*	ah kay **oh**-rah
Just a moment.	*Un momento.*	oon moh-**mayn**-toh
now / soon / later	*adesso / presto / tardi*	ah-**dehs**-soh / **prehs**-toh / **tar**-dee
today / tomorrow	*oggi / domani*	**oh**-jee / doh-**mah**-nee

In an Italian-speaking Restaurant

English	Italian	Pronunciation
I'd like...	*Vorrei...*	vor-**rehee**
We'd like...	*Vorremmo...*	vor-**ray**-moh
...to reserve...	*...prenotare...*	pray-noh-**tah**-ray
...a table for one / two.	*...un tavolo per uno / due.*	oon **tah**-voh-loh pehr **oo**-noh / **doo**-ay
Non-smoking.	*Non fumare.*	nohn foo-**mah**-ray
Is this seat free?	*È libero questo posto?*	eh **lee**-bay-roh **kwehs**-toh **poh**-stoh
The menu (in English), please.	*Il menù (in inglese), per favore.*	eel may-**noo** (een een-**glay**-zay) pehr fah-**voh**-ray
service (not) included	*servizio (non) incluso*	sehr-**veet**-seeoh (nohn) een-**kloo**-zoh
cover charge	*pane e coperto*	**pah**-nay ay koh-**pehr**-toh
to go	*da portar via*	dah **por**-tar **vee**-ah
with / without	*con / senza*	kohn / **sehn**-sah
and / or	*e / o*	ay / oh
menu (of the day)	*menù (del giorno)*	may-**noo** (dayl **jor**-noh)
specialty of the house	*specialità della casa*	spay-chah-lee-**tah dehl**-lah **kah**-zah
first course (pasta, soup)	*primo piatto*	**pree**-moh peeah-toh
main course (meat, fish)	*secondo piatto*	say-**kohn**-doh peeah-toh
side dishes	*contorni*	kohn-**tor**-nee
bread	*pane*	**pah**-nay
cheese	*formaggio*	for-**mah**-joh
sandwich	*panino*	pah-**nee**-noh
soup	*minestra, zuppa*	mee-**nehs**-trah, **tsoo**-pah
salad	*insalata*	een-sah-**lah**-tah
meat	*carne*	**kar**-nay
chicken	*pollo*	**poh**-loh
fish	*pesce*	**peh**-shay
seafood	*frutti di mare*	**froo**-tee day **mah**-ray
fruit / vegetables	*frutta / legumi*	**froo**-tah / lay-**goo**-mee
dessert	*dolci*	**dohl**-chee
tap water	*acqua del rubinetto*	**ah**-kwah dayl roo-bee-**nay**-toh
mineral water	*acqua minerale*	**ah**-kwah mee-nay-**rah**-lay
milk	*latte*	**lah**-tay
(orange) juice	*succo (d'arancia)*	**soo**-koh (dah-**rahn**-chah)
coffee / tea	*caffè / tè*	kah-**feh** / teh
wine	*vino*	**vee**-noh
red / white	*rosso / bianco*	**roh**-soh / bee**ahn**-koh
glass / bottle	*bicchiere / bottiglia*	bee-kee**ay**-ray / boh-**teel**-yah
beer	*birra*	**bee**-rah
Cheers!	*Cin cin!*	cheen cheen
More. / Another.	*Ancora un po.' / Un altro.*	ahn-**koh**-rah oon poh / oon **ahl**-troh
The same.	*Lo stesso.*	loh **stehs**-soh
The bill, please.	*Il conto, per favore.*	eel **kohn**-toh pehr fah-**voh**-ray
tip	*mancia*	**mahn**-chah
Delicious!	*Delizioso!*	day-leet-see**oh**-zoh

For more user-friendly Italian phrases, check out *Rick Steves' Italian Phrase Book & Dictionary* or *Rick Steves' French, Italian, and German Phrase Book.*

INDEX

INDEX

Explore Europe

At ricksteves.com you can browse through thousands of articles, videos, photos and radio interviews, plus find a wealth of money-saving travel tips for planning your dream trip. And with our mobile-friendly website, you can easily access all this great travel information anywhere you go.

TV Shows

Preview the places you'll visit by watching entire half-hour episodes of Rick Steves' Europe (choose from all 100 shows) on-demand, for free.

ricksteves.com

your travel dreams into affordable reality

Radio Interviews

Enjoy ready access to Rick's vast library of radio interviews covering travel

tips and cultural insights that relate specifically to your Europe travel plans.

Travel Forums

Learn, ask, share! Our online community of savvy travelers is a great resource for first-time travelers to Europe, as well as seasoned pros. You'll find forums on each country, plus travel tips and restaurant/hotel reviews. You can even ask one of our well-traveled staff to chime in with an opinion.

Travel News

Subscribe to our free Travel News e-newsletter, and get monthly updates from Rick on what's happening in Europe.

Audio Europe™

Rick's Free Travel App

Get your FREE **Rick Steves Audio Europe**™ app to enjoy…

- Dozens of self-guided tours of Europe's top museums, sights and historic walks

- Hundreds of tracks filled with cultural insights and sightseeing tips from Rick's radio interviews

- All organized into handy geographic playlists

- For iPhone, iPad, iPod Touch, Android

With Rick whispering in your ear, Europe gets even better.

Find out more at ricksteves.com

Gear up for your next adventure at ricksteves.com

Light Luggage

Pack light and right with Rick Steves' affordable, custom-designed rolling carry-on bags, backpacks, day packs and shoulder bags.

Accessories

From packing cubes to moneybelts and beyond, Rick has personally selected the travel goodies that will help your trip go smoother.

Rick Steves has

Experience maximum Europe

Save time and energy

This guidebook is your independent-travel toolkit. But for all it delivers, it's still up to you to devote the time and energy it takes to manage the preparation and logistics that are essential for a happy trip. If that's a hassle, there's a solution.

Rick Steves Tours

A Rick Steves tour takes you to Europe's most interesting places with great

great tours, too!

with minimum stress

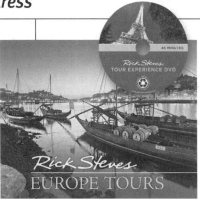

guides and small groups of 28 or less. We follow Rick's favorite itineraries, ride in comfy buses, stay in family-run hotels, and bring you intimately close to the Europe you've traveled so far to see. Most importantly, we take away the logistical headaches so you can focus on the fun.

customers—along with us on 40 different itineraries, from Ireland to Italy to Istanbul. Is a Rick Steves tour the right fit for your travel dreams? Find out at ricksteves.com, where you can also get Rick's latest tour catalog and free Tour Experience DVD.

Join the fun

This year we'll take 18,000 free-spirited travelers— nearly half of them repeat

Europe is best experienced with happy travel partners. We hope you can join us.

See our itineraries at ricksteves.com

Rick Steves

Rick Steves guidebooks are published by Avalon Travel, a member of the Perseus Books Group.

Maximize your travel skills with a good guidebook.

Avalon Travel
a member of the Perseus Books Group
1700 Fourth Street
Berkeley, CA 94710

Printed in Canada by Friesens
First printing December 2015

ISBN 978-1-63121-199-7

For the latest on Rick's lectures, guidebooks, tours, public radio show, and public television series, contact Rick Steves' Europe, Inc., 130 Fourth Avenue North, Edmonds, WA 98020, tel. 425/771-8303, www.ricksteves.com, rick@ricksteves.com.

Rick Steves' Europe
Special Publications Manager: Risa Laib
Managing Editor: Jennifer Madison Davis
Editors: Glenn Eriksen, Tom Griffin, Katherine Gustafson, Suzanne Kotz, Cathy Lu, John Pierce, Carrie Shepherd
Editorial & Production Assistant: Jessica Shaw
Editorial Intern: Shirley Qiu
Researchers: Virginia Agostinelli, Ben Cameron, Trish Feaster, Cameron Hewitt, Suzanne Kotz
Contributor: Gene Openshaw
Maps & Graphics: David C. Hoerlein, Sandra Hundacker, Lauren Mills, Mary Rostad

Avalon Travel
Senior Editor and Series Manager: Madhu Prasher
Editor: Jamie Andrade
Associate Editor: Maggie Ryan
Copy Editors: Judith Brown and Suzie Nasol
Proofreader: Denise Silva
Indexer: Stephen Callahan
Production and Typesetting: Rue Flaherty, Tabitha Lahr
Cover Design: Kimberly Glyder Design
Maps & Graphics: Kat Bennett, Mike Morgenfeld

Photo Credits
Front Cover: Amalfi Cathedral © Jennifer Barrow | Dreamstime.com
Title Page Photo: Piazza del Plebiscito, Naples, Italy © edella/www.123rf.com
Additional Photography: Dominic Bonuccelli, Ben Cameron, Jennifer Hauseman, Cameron Hewitt, David C. Hoerlein, Anne Jenkins, Gene Openshaw, Michael Potter, Robyn Stencil, Rick Steves, Bruce VanDeventer, Laura VanDeventer, Les Wahlstrom, Ian Watson, Wikimedia Commons

ABOUT THE AUTHOR

RICK STEVES

 Since 1973, Rick Steves has spent 100 days every year exploring Europe. Along with writing and researching a bestselling series of guidebooks, Rick produces a public television series *(Rick Steves' Europe)*, a public radio show *(Travel with Rick Steves)*, a blog (on Facebook), and an app and podcast *(Rick Steves Audio Europe)*; writes a nationally syndicated newspaper column; organizes guided tours that take over 20,000 travelers to Europe annually; and offers an information-packed website (www.ricksteves.com). With the help of his hardworking staff of 100 at Rick Steves' Europe—in Edmonds, Washington, just north of Seattle—Rick's mission is to make European travel fun, affordable, and culturally enlightening for Americans.

Connect with Rick:

facebook.com/RickSteves   twitter: @RickSteves

instagram: ricksteveseurope

Want More Italy?
Maximize the experience with Rick Steves as your guide

Guidebooks
Venice, Florence, and Rome guides make side-trips smooth and affordable

Phrase Books
Rely on Rick's Italian Phrase Book and Dictionary

Rick's DVDs
Preview where you're going with 15 shows on Italy

Free! Rick's Audio Europe™ App
Get free audio tours for Italy's top sights

Small-Group Tours
Rick offers a dozen great itineraries through Italy

For all the details, visit ricksteves.com